D1644974

WITHDRAWN FROM
CHRIST CHURCH LIBRARY
OXFORD

Christ Church

T019016

THE SCHWEICH LECTURES ON
BIBLICAL ARCHAEOLOGY, 1942

SOME HELLENISTIC
ELEMENTS IN PRIMITIVE
CHRISTIANITY

Some Hellenistic Elements in Primitive Christianity

BY

WILFRED L. KNOX, D.D.

Hon. Canon of Ely, Chaplain of Pembroke College, Cambridge
Formerly Scholar of Trinity College, Oxford

THE SCHWEICH LECTURES
OF THE BRITISH ACADEMY
1942

LONDON
PUBLISHED FOR THE BRITISH ACADEMY
BY HUMPHREY MILFORD, OXFORD UNIVERSITY PRESS
AMEN HOUSE, E.C. 4
1944

OXFORD UNIVERSITY PRESS
AMEN HOUSE, E.C. 4
LONDON EDINBURGH GLASGOW NEW YORK
TORONTO MELBOURNE CAPETOWN BOMBAY
CALCUTTA MADRAS
HUMPHREY MILFORD
PUBLISHER TO THE UNIVERSITY

PRINTED IN GREAT BRITAIN

PREFACE

I HAVE learnt so much at the Seminar formerly conducted by the late Professor F. C. Burkitt and since his death by Professor C. H. Dodd that I feel bound to acknowledge here my debt to them and to my fellow-members. I have endeavoured in these lectures and the notes to acknowledge particular borrowings; where I have failed to do so by inadvertence I trust that the lenders will forgive me.

My thanks are also due to the Rev. H. M. Chadwick for his assistance in correcting the proofs.

WILFRED L. KNOX

PEMBROKE COLLEGE
CAMBRIDGE
October 6, 1943

ABBREVIATIONS

Beginnings.	*The Beginnings of Christianity*, ed. Foakes Jackson and Kirsopp Lake.
F.G.H.	*Die Fragmente der griechischen Historiker*, ed. A. Jacoby.
Gr.N.T.Gr.	Blass's *Grammar of New Testament Greek*, tr. Thackeray (1905 ed.).
H.T.R.	*Harvard Theological Review.*
L.S.J.	*Liddell and Scott's Greek-English Lexicon*, ed. by H. H. Stuart Jones.
P.M.G.	*Papyri Magicae Graecae*, ed. Preisendanz.
P.W.K.	*Pauly's Realencyclopädie der classischen Altertumswissenschaft*, ed. G. Wissowa and W. Kroll.
T.W.z.N.T	*Theologisches Wörterbuch zum neuen Testament*, ed. G. Kittel.
Voc. Gr. N.T.	*Vocabulary of the Greek New Testament*, by J. H. Moulton and G. Milligan.

I have referred to my books *St. Paul and the Church of Jerusalem* and *St. Paul and the Church of the Gentiles* as *Jerusalem* and *Gentiles* respectively.

CONTENTS

LECTURE I

THE object of these lectures is to study some of the methods by which the Gospel preached by Jesus in Galilee, a remote backwater of an insignificant Roman province, was converted into a system that could gain a hearing in the civilized world and could end by conquering it. The hellenization of the Gospel was inevitable. It is arguable that the Church took a wrong turning when it substituted for the human teacher Jesus of Nazareth the figure of a glorified Messiah, shortly to return on the clouds of heaven. But this step had already been taken long before any of our records were written: the worship of Jesus goes back to the beginning of Christianity. Judaism was not a theological religion, and Jewish Christians could be content to worship Jesus as Lord without asking how such worship could be reconciled with the monotheism of Israel. But the Gospel must be preached to all the world; it had therefore to be translated into the Greek language and accommodated to the general theological conceptions of the hellenistic world, and worked out into a coherent scheme of thought: in what follows I hope to consider some of the writings in which the task was accomplished.

We must begin with one or two preliminary cautions. The miraculous element in the N.T. does not reflect the infiltration of alien ideas into a simple Jewish ethical movement. Miracles were as much at home in the mental climate of Palestine as anywhere else. If we look at the story of the widow's son at Nain (Lk. 7. 11) we find in it a miracle far more remarkable than the general run of synoptic miracles; and it is recorded only by the most hellenized of the synoptic writers. We might suppose that the author invented it to gratify the Greek public's love of wonders. Unfortunately the author can write quite good Greek when he chooses. But this story, as Greek, is a sheer atrocity. It consists of a string of short sentences; out of 16 conjunctions, 12 are καί and the other 4 δέ; the Hebrew-Aramaic suffix is represented by an unnecessary Greek personal pronoun 8 times in some 4 verses. It is, in other words, a typical bit of bad translation-Greek, even worse than the average. It is certainly not invented by Luke; whether true or not, it is part of his Palestinian tradition.

The point is of some importance in view of the tendency to ascribe any part of the Gospels which we dislike to 'hellenistic influences'. An obvious instance is the story of the virgin birth of Jesus. Now the story may or may not be true. If you do not believe it, it is convenient to ascribe it to alien influences, using the stories of the miraculous birth of Plato, Alexander the Great, or Julius Caesar as parallels. You can even derive it from the religion of ancient Egypt, mediated through Philo's frigid allegories in which God's intercourse with the soul makes it a virgin, which yet produces the offspring of virtue. I can only say that this view seems to me the most improbable explanation imaginable. As a matter of fact Judaism was quite used to infancy legends; the rabbis love to dilate on the miracle involved in the birth of Isaac in view of the old age of his parents; the O.T. has several miraculous births, such as those of Samson and Samuel, which look like legends attached to the local shrines of Palestine modified and adopted by Israelite tradition.[1] If the story be a legend, I see no reason to suppose that it is not a legend native to the soil of Palestine.

Again, we must be careful not to distinguish 'Palestinian' and 'hellenistic' Judaism as if there were a complete cleavage between the two. There is of course a vast gulf between the most and the least hellenized elements of Judaism at the beginning of our era, between for example Philo and the Mishnah. But the difference is one of mental climate, not of geography. Josephus, apart from a short visit to Rome, was Palestinian in origin and education[2]; but it is very hard to suppose that he acquired all his Greek culture after the fall of Jerusalem. On the other hand, the sixth satire of Juvenal shows us a Judaism at Rome, which may have spoken a barbarous kind of Greek, but has no trace of Greek culture; it observes the Torah and combines with it a purely Jewish practice of magic.[3] Even in the remoter parts of Galilee there was some contact with Greek; after all, one of Jesus' disciples bore the name of Philip. On the other hand, the most hellenized Jew of Alexandria, unless he deliberately changed his religion, was primarily a Jew. Philo is by far the most hellenized Jew known to us; but he is always a Jew for whom the Torah is far more important than his superficial dabblings in philosophy. Within these limits we have an infinite number of variations. In general it can hardly be denied that the sources which lie behind the Synoptic Gospels are redolent of the soil of Palestine; it is the most striking testimony to the value of the synoptic tradition that though it reaches us through the Churches of the Greek world, it gives us a story which could only have happened in this remote backwater.

[1] See Note to this lecture.   [2] Vita, 7 ff.
[3] Juv. Sat. 6. 542 ff.

How small the Greek element is can best be seen by looking at some passages where it is very clearly marked; we can even find them in the Marcan narrative.

The most remarkable instance is the words of Jesus in the garden of Gethsemane in Mk. 14. 38. Jesus comes to His disciples; after the words 'Simon, sleepest thou?' He breaks into a perfect piece of artificial prose of the popular rhetorical type described in Norden's great work *Die antike Kunstprosa*. We have a series of short clauses, the first three balancing one another in length, with a similar balance between the last two; four of the five have correct rhythmical endings (γρηγορῆσαι $[-\cup|-\cup]$, καὶ προσεύχεσθε $[-\cup-|-\cup]$, πνεῦμα πρόθυμον $[-\cup|\underset{\cup\cup}{}\cup]$, ἡ δὲ σάρξ ἀσθενής $[-\cup-|-\cup-]$. The passage includes a contrast of μέν and δέ, which is very rare in Mark (about 4 times in all), and a quite Pauline contrast of spirit and flesh as the sources of good and evil. There may lie behind the narrative a good tradition of what Jesus actually said; but it comes to us in a form which seems to be derived from a Christian homily which possessed a standard of Greek as good as any in the N.T.

Thus we cannot rule out hellenistic influences from Mark. For another case we may look at the stories of the miraculous feeding of the multitudes. Clearly Mk. 8. 1–10 (the 4,000) is a doublet of Mk. 6. 35 ff. (the 5,000). But how did the doublets come into being with just this trifling discrepancy in the numbers involved? The explanation seems to lie in the curious fact that while in Mk. 6. 41 Jesus 'blesses' the bread (εὐλόγησεν), in 8. 6 He 'gives thanks' (εὐχαριστήσας). Now the word εὐχαριστεῖν and its derivatives only appear rather late in Greek literature,[1] with a rather formal connotation, often of a religious kind.[2] On the other hand, Hebrew has no word which simply means to thank in our sense of 'saying thank you'; the word meaning to 'bless' can be used of thanking God or man (as in 2 Sam. 14. 22), and man can thank God in words meaning to praise, to acknowledge, to magnify, to extol, or to glorify[3]; the levitical sacrifices of thanksgiving are properly sacrifices of acknowledgement. The LXX translators of the Hebrew Bible had thus no need to use the word. In later Greek the word loses any formal

[1] The earliest reference in LSJ. is a decree in Demosth. 18. 92.
[2] Cf. Posidonius *ap.* Athenaeus 5. 213 *e* (a vote of thanks); Diod. Sic. 29. 11 (missions of thanks); 2 Macc. 12. 45 (a votive tablet); Polyb. 5. 14. 8 (a sacrifice of thanksgiving).
[3] αἰνῶν (הלל), ἐξομολογοῦμαι (ידה), μεγαλύνω (גדל), δοξάζω (כבד), and εὐλογῶν (ברך) are the commonest words.

religious sense[1]; at the same time it begins to appear in Jewish Greek; we find it, though rarely, in the Greek versions of the apocryphal books[2]; by the time of Philo it is frequent, and has a marked tendency to be associated with liturgical thanksgivings,[3] as it has also in Josephus.[4] By the time of Aquila's translation the word was so well acclimatized that it is used with some frequency, with a noticeable tendency to a liturgical meaning.[5]

The N.T. represents a definite stage in this development. St. Paul uses the word freely, and his use is that of the hellenistic world.[6] But in the synoptic tradition the use of the word is confined (except for two exceptions to be noted later in Luke) to the Last Supper[7] and to this second version of the miracle of feeding in Mark and its Matthean parallel. Now Mark had no need to use the word in his narrative of the Last Supper; he is quite indifferent to style and could perfectly well have repeated εὐλόγησεν. His use of the term at the Last Supper implies that his story has passed through circles in which the term was regularly used of the eucharist as the εὐχαριστήριος θυσία of the Church,[8] and these can only have been circles in which there was a strong hellenistic influence. In the case of the miracle of feeding it would seem that the first version, the feeding of the 5,000, represents the original semitic version of the story; the

[1] In the ordinary sense of 'gratitude' it appears in a list of virtues attributed to Chrysippus by Andronicus of Rhodes (c. 50 B.C.); cf. St. vet. Frr. 3. 67 (273).

[2] Normally of thanking God, but in Ecclus. 37. 11 of the virtue of gratitude; in 2 Macc. 2. 27 of the thanks of one man to another.

[3] For its religious use cf. especially Q.D.S.I. 8 f.; De Spec. Legg. 1. 224. For its use of thanking men cf. In Flacc. 98 and 100, where, however, we are dealing with the more or less formal thanks of subjects to rulers.

[4] Cf. Antt. 2. 346 of Moses' ode of praise and thanksgiving (somewhat startlingly 'in hexameter verse') composed after the 'salvation' wrought by God through His 'epiphany' at the Red Sea (presumably from Nicolas of Damascus).

[5] Nine times according to Hatch and Redpath, notably of the 'sacrifice of thanksgiving' in Lev. 7. 12; cf. Ps. 107. 22 and Amos. 4. 5. Some other passages suggest a liturgical use of the Psalter. It should be remembered that Aquila's version claimed to be more literal than the LXX; it follows that the word and the idea were by this time quite acclimatized.

[6] Normally of thanking God, but of thanking men in Ro. 16. 4. No doubt his insistence on thanksgiving reflects the fervent enthusiasm of the primitive Church; but 1 Peter, which is scarcely less enthusiastic and written in better Greek, uses 'glorify', 'glory', and 'praise'.

[7] Of the Cup in Mk. 14. 23, Mt. 26. 27, and Lk. 22. 17; also in Lk. 22. 19 of the Bread.

[8] As it is in the Didache, 9. 1 ff. and 14. 1.

later, the feeding of the 4,000, is the hellenized version, in which the miraclc has already been recognized as a type of the eucharist as it is in the Fourth Gospel, where somewhat significantly the εὐλογήσας of Mark is replaced by εὐχαριστήσας.[1]

There is one more place at which Mark seems to have incorporated a passage which has passed through a hellenistic channel. In Mark 7 we have a dispute between Jesus and the Pharisees on eating meat with unwashed hands. It is introduced by an account of the Pharisaic attitude, whereas elsewhere in Mark it is assumed that the Pharisaic attitude is familiar to the reader. It culminates in a speech by Jesus, giving a long category of the vices which 'come out' from a man and so defile him. Such a catalogue is entirely different from any other part of the teaching of Jesus as it has been preserved; but it is entirely in keeping with the practice of the hellenistic synagogue,[2] a practice which was borrowed from Greek philosophy. There is no reason to doubt that Jesus said that it is not the things which go into a man but the things which come out from him that defile him, and such a saying would naturally be preserved by the Church in its controversies with the Jews. But it looks

---

[1] Jno. 6. 11 and 23. It also appears of thanking God in Jno. 11. 41. For the sake of completeness it may be noted that the term is not employed in Heb. (whose author writes excellent Greek), while it appears three times in the Apocalypse in spite of the author's hebraizing style. The fact suggests that this style, which, where not due to an incorporation of sources, seems intended to read as an imitation of Hebrew as the correct language of prophecy, breaks down at this point.

[2] Wisd. 14. 22 ff.; Ps.-Heraclitus Ep. 7. 35 ff. (for the Jewish origin of this cf. Bernays, *Die heraklitischen Briefe*, 72); Ro. 1. 28 ff.; 1 Cor. 6. 9 ff.; Gal. 5. 19 ff. It may be observed that Str.-B. on Mt. 15 (= Mk. 7) give no parallel for this list of vices from rabbinical sources; the systematic hebdomad of vices quoted from Derek Erets Zuta 7 is entirely different in form and worked out to suit Prov. 26. 25.

The most portentous specimen of the type is Philo, De Sacr. Ab. et Cain. 20 ff., going back ultimately to the Choice of Heracles, which first appears in Xen. Mem. 2. 1. 21 ff.; it has passed through several hands before reaching Philo. The virtues which accompany one of the two women and the vices which accompany the other are given at enormous length; the vices amount to about 150. The vices are described as 'the great mysteries' of pleasure; Bréhier, *Idées philosophiques de Philon*, 39 ff., compares the 'mythography' of the Tabula of Cebes. For the whole passage cf. Wendland, *Neuentdeckte Fragmente Philos*, 140, who holds that Philo's immediate source is Epicurean. For other catalogues of the kind cf. Epict. Diss. 2. 16. 45; Corp. Herm. 9. 3. The tradition goes back at least as far as Cleanthes, whose description of the good (Clem. Alex. Protr. 6. 72 (61 P) implies an opposed list of vices; cf. Stob. Ecl. 2. 7. 11g, Wachsm. p. 100.

suspiciously as though the long explanation with its list of vices represents a fragment of the controversy of the Church with the synagogue; it is even possible that we can reconstruct the other side. For Plato says the exact opposite: the mouth is designed for the entrance of what is necessary, but for the exit of what is best,[1] a passage which Philo interprets[2] of the entrance of the perishable food of the perishable body, but the exit of words, the immortal laws of the immortal soul. Philo is not here referring to the Jewish food-taboos, but it was a commonplace that the food-laws of Moses were intended to inculcate moral precepts.[3] I suspect that hellenistic Jews quoted Plato against Jesus.

In these passages we seem to have fairly clear evidence of the influence of hellenistic thought and speech going back behind the Marcan tradition. But it must be remembered that the tradition had been circulating in oral form in the Greek world for some thirty years; it speaks much for its reliability that it remains on the whole so thoroughly semitic.[4] Of the other two synoptic Gospels Matthew need not detain us. We may suspect that his story contains a good deal of legendary accretion, but his accretions are purely Jewish, or at least oriental, motifs which need never have passed through a Greek medium.[5] We may, however, note in passing that the famous logion Mt. 11. 25 = Lk. 10. 21 ff., 'I thank thee, O Father, Lord of heaven and earth', sometimes treated as 'hellenistic', is purely semitic in its use of ἐξομολογοῦμαι for εὐχαριστῶ, and the whole structure of

---

[1] Timaeus 75 e.   [2] De Mund. Op. 119.

[3] Aristeas, 143 ff. The Pythagoreans treated their master's taboos in the same way: Diog. Laert. 8. 34; Plut. De Lib. Educ. (2) 17. 12 d.

[4] There is a curious instance of purely verbal influence in Mk. 3. 5 f. There seems to be no parallel for συλλυπούμενος in the sense of 'being grieved'. It means 'to sympathize'. Bultmann in *T.W.z.N.T.* 4. 325 treats it as an emphatic form, but gives no parallels. But *contristari* in this sense is good Latin as early as Seneca (Ep. 85. 14). We might have here an isolated instance of a Latin influence on the *koine*, the lack of parallels being due to chance. But the same story contains the word συμβούλιον for which again there is no parallel in the sense of 'counsel' as against 'council'. But it is a very natural translation of the Latin *consilium*. Two latinisms, both *hapax legomena* in their sense, in one pericope suggests that the story has passed from Greek (or Aramaic) into Latin and back into Greek before it reached its place in Mark.

[5] The repentance and suicide of Judas are fulfilments of *testimonia*; for Pilate's wife and his washing of his hands cf. Str.-B. ad locc. For the implied descent into Hades cf. Kroll, *Gott u. Hölle*, 6 ff.; for the Infancy narrative cf. Note to this lecture.

the sentences is semitic.[1] Such 'acknowledgements' of thanks to God arc common in the O.T.,[2] while the thought that man's knowledge of God is due to a previous 'knowing' of him by God is admittedly an oriental and semitic conception.[3] It may be admitted that there is a remarkable similarity between the logion and some hellenistic utterances, but this is due to the fact that it is cast in a form which was borrowed by the Greeks from the semitic world.[4] The saying may or may not be an authentic utterance of Jesus; but if we reject it, it must be on the grounds of our general attitude to the person of Jesus, not on the ground that its form or language are 'hellenistic' in any intelligible sense.

Luke, whose Gospel must be taken in conjunction with its continuation in the Acts of the Apostles, is entirely different. He claims in his preface to be writing as a scientific historian, and he tries to fit the chronology of the Gospel into world-history; but it must be admitted that here his claim to be regarded as an historian ends. He is simply a compiler, who had at his disposal a peculiarly semitic infancy story, Mark, Q, a large block of matter peculiar to himself,[5] some additional material about the history of the Passion from another source than Mark (or invented by himself), a narrative of the resurrection appearances, a story of the Church in Jerusalem from a very semitic source, an account of St. Paul's missionary activities written on the whole in much better Greek, and his own travel-diary,

[1] Cf. Creed, *The Gospel according to St. Luke*, ad loc., for the semitic use of parataxis and of ἔμπροσθέν σου to avoid the familiarity of σοί.

[2] Cf. 2 Sam. 22. 50; Dan. 2. 23; Tobit 13. 6; Ps. 9. 1, and the Psalms *passim*.

[3] Jer. 1. 5; Amos 3. 2, where God's knowledge is an act of selection calling man to God's service; for man as knowing God cf. Jer. 31. 34. For the whole conception cf. *Gentiles*, 122, n. 3. Bultmann in *T.W.z.N.T.* 1. 692 ff. distinguishes between Greek, Gnostic, and Jewish conceptions of Gnosis, and holds (ib. 713) that the use here, as in the Fourth Gospel, is 'gnostic', implying mystical or ecstatic contemplation; but he admits (ib. 702) that Philo fluctuates between the different conceptions, and the same applies to the N.T., where it is impossible to pin the writers down to a specific meaning, especially in such a matter as the 'knowledge of God', where precision is impossible.

[4] Norden, *Agnostos Theos*, 277 ff., derives the utterance and Ecclus. 51. 1 ff. from a common type of solemn religious utterance of mixed Greek and oriental origin taken over by hellenized Judaism from the orientalized Stoicism of Posidonius. It is probable enough that both utterances are modelled on a similar pattern; the resemblances are too close to be fortuitous. But the pattern seems to be the traditional thanksgiving of semitic religion, of which the O.T. contains numerous specimens; the borrowing seems to have been entirely on the Greek side.

[5] i.e. the bulk of the 'great insertion', 9. 51–18. 14.

conflated with the Pauline story at the appropriate points. Like many other ancient writers he is mainly concerned with the amalgamation of pre-existing materials.

He was, however, writing for a Greek public with some education, and had to do something to improve the barbarous form of those materials; his most obvious improvements are the introduction of Attic words, the omission of barbarous ones, and the removal of superfluous pronouns representing the Aramaic suffix.[1] Even so he is amazingly careless; an amusing instance can be seen by comparing Lk. 3.16 with Acts 13.25. Both are the Baptist's saying 'There comes one after me the latchet of whose shoes I am not worthy to unloose'. In his Gospel Luke copies Mark and writes οὗ οὐκ εἰμὶ ἱκανὸς λῦσαι τὸν ἱμάντα τῶν ὑποδημάτων αὐτοῦ without troubling to remove the bad αὐτοῦ at the end. In the latter he is reproducing the typical apostolic form of preaching in which a summary of the O.T. leads up to a brief summary of the Gospel story.[2] He may be composing a 'Thucydidean' speech, but it corresponds to a form which is stereotyped in our documents and was probably quite largely stereotyped in practice. He may have heard St. Paul deliver a sermon of the kind, quoting the Baptist, on more than one occasion. In any case, the offending αὐτοῦ at the end is omitted, because it was not in his source. Again, he has made a gallant attempt to get rid of the barbaric word 'Amen' in the sense of 'truly'; Matthew has it 30 times, which Luke has reduced to 7; but the 7 remain. It is probable that his attempts to improve the style of his materials were not a little hampered by his own knowledge of the LXX[3] and by his familiarity with the religious vocabulary of the primitive Church, which must have been vilely semitic.[4]

[1] For a full study of these and similar points cf. Creed's admirable commentary, pp. lxxvi ff.

[2] For the kerygma as a more or less conventional and stereotyped form cf. Dodd, *The Apostolic Preaching and its Developments*, 57 ff.

[3] Cf. Creed, loc. cit. lxxviii.

[4] For Luke's tendency to follow an Aramaic source (whether a document written in Aramaic or an informant who talked translation-Greek) more closely than Matthew, who uses a relative freedom in translating language which he understands while Luke does not, cf. Kittel, 'Die Probleme des pal. Spätjudenthums u. d. Urchristenthums' in *Beitr. z. Wiss. vom alt. u. neu. Test.* 3. 51 ff. Luke's own writing is not entirely above criticism, e.g. the second αὐτῷ in Acts 20. 16 is very clumsy. In 28. 8 ἐπιθεὶς τὰς χεῖρας αὐτῷ ἰάσατο αὐτόν is atrocious, but here we have the language of the Church in describing miracles as standardized by Mark. Acts 20. 10 is a similar case of almost technical language in describing miracles, if it is not a verbatim report of Paul's words, which is perfectly possible.

In general, however, he shows a remarkable fidelity to his sources; as an instance we can go back to his use of the word εὐχαριστεῖν. He gets through his infancy narrative, including the four great εὐχαριστήριοι ὕμνοι of primitive Christianity, without using it once. He uses it in his narrative of the Last Supper (22. 17 and 19), in the rather enigmatic story of the meal just before St. Paul's shipwreck (Acts 27. 35), also at 28. 15 and in the opening of the speech of Tertullus in Acts 24. 3. So far we might have a consistent avoidance of the word, as having no Hebrew equivalent, except as a term for the eucharist or in quite definitely Greek surroundings. But we find it twice in the long insertion in his Gospel, the story of the ten lepers (17. 16) and in the parable of the Pharisee and the Publican (18. 11). Here we are in an entirely Palestinian atmosphere and the word is quite inappropriate; the explanation both of its use here and its non-use elsewhere seems to be that Luke was often content to copy out his sources faithfully and was a very slovenly corrector. In support of this it may be noted that in his long insertion he has three times preserved the rabbinical use of the third person plural as a reverential periphrasis for the direct mention of God; the use would be entirely unintelligible to Gentile readers.[1] On the other hand, from time to time we find alterations in which Luke betrays himself by a use of Greek which shines like a good deed in a naughty world both in the Gospel and in the Acts.

(1) Apart from the Preface the first is Lk. 2. 1–5, which is excellent Greek except that ἐγένετο followed by a main verb is inferior to its use with the infinitive (= συνέβη), but here Luke may have been affected by the frequent use of the inferior form in his sources. ἐπορεύοντο ἕκαστος εἰς τὴν ἑαυτοῦ πόλιν, is good classical Greek; the whole story is told with only four main verbs, thanks to a competent use of subordinate clauses; there is only one superfluous αὐτῷ (v. 5). But at v. 6 we relapse into a riot

---

[1] 6. 38 'they' shall give into your bosom, 12. 20 this night 'they' demand thy soul back from thee, 16. 9 that 'they' may receive you into everlasting habitations. 12. 48 may be another instance, but here 'men' would make good sense. Creed on 6. 38 treats the phrase as equivalent to the passive, but this ignores the established rabbinical usage, for which cf. Mishnah, Yôma, 8. 9 (Danby 172, but the translation 'he will be given' does not do justice to the idiom; for this cf. Montefiore and Loewe, A Rabbinical Anthology, 179. n. 1). The general colouring of these passages is entirely semitic, as is that of the passages in which εὐχαριστεῖν occurs; it is perhaps interesting to note that the use of this word which is almost peculiar to St. Paul in the N.T. should be combined with a rabbinical usage with which he must have been familiar, though he avoids it in his letters to Gentile converts.

of parataxis and semitic pronouns. Now it would seem that there were two traditions current from quite early times; one represented Nazareth as the birthplace of Jesus (cf. Mt. 2. 23, John 1. 45 and 7. 52), the other Bethlehem, which was necessary if the prophecies were to be fulfilled (Mt. 2. 6 and 17). I fear that Luke has harmonized the two traditions by the expedient of the census.[1]

(2) We have a similar passage in Lk. 7. 2–8, the healing of the centurion's servant from Q. Luke has rewritten the story by introducing the centurion's Jewish piety and the support of his request by the elders of the Jews. The story reached him in the form that he sent messengers instead of coming himself: ἀπέστειλεν πρὸς αὐτὸν . . . ἐρωτῶν αὐτὸν . . . τὸν δοῦλον αὐτοῦ shows a semitic original which has survived, whereas in v. 2 (a model sentence) he has eliminated the unnecessary pronoun three times as compared with Mt. 8. 5. He narrates the whole incident with only five main verbs by his better knowledge of syntax; the fact that the centurion sends friends instead of coming himself makes it necessary to introduce the sentence διὸ οὐδὲ ἐμαυτὸν ἠξίωσα πρός σε ἐλθεῖν, which is good classical Greek. The effect of his changes is that the centurion becomes the representative of that large number of Gentile converts who arrived at Christianity through an earlier attachment to the synagogue; it seems that Luke has rewritten the story in order to introduce a prototype of this class into the life of Jesus.[2]

(3) At 17. 28 Luke has added to the saying about the days of Noah another saying about the days of Lot, thus adapting the original saying to the hellenistic tradition (going back to the Timaeus) that the world is visited at intervals by alternate catastrophes of flood and fire. Hellenistic Judaism delighted in

---

[1] For the problems connected with the census cf. Creed, ad loc.; he sees (p. 30) a dramatic appropriateness in the coincidence of the birth with the imperial decree. But Josephus (Antt. 18. 4 ff. and B. J. 2. 118) attaches the revolt of Judas and the rise of the Zealot movement to the census of Quirinus, and I am inclined to suspect that Luke had a tradition which assigned the birth of Jesus to the same period on the ground of appropriateness, though Luke himself did not realize it. Cf. Acts 5. 36 f., where Luke wrongly places Theudas before Judas; there would be far more point in Gamaliel's speech if it were supposed that the birth of Jesus coincided with the rebellion of Judas.

[2] For the tendency of Roman soldiers to adopt the religion of the country where they served cf. Tac. Hist. 3. 24; for a synagogue built by a pagan official cf. Dittenberger, O.G.I.S. 96 quoted by Creed, ad loc. Verse 7 is omitted by D and some Western texts; for its retention cf. Creed, ad loc. The Greek is far too good for an interpolator.

the theme as proving the truth of the O.T.[1] Luke introduces
the theme in excellent rhetorical prose; the days of Noah are
described in four verbs making a tetracolon with asyndeton, the
days of Lot in a tricolon, where each colon consists of two verbs,
with asyndeton; both accounts end with 'and destroyed them
all' to give assonance.[2]

(4) A remarkable passage of this type is Lk. 22. 68, where
Jesus is represented not as being silent in the face of His accusers,
but as entering an almost formal refusal to plead in the four short
and well-balanced clauses ἐὰν ὑμῖν εἴπω | οὐ μὴ πιστεύσητε | ἐὰν
Δὲ ἐρωτήσω | οὐ μὴ ἀποκριθῆτε where the assonance amounts to
rhyme.[3] The reason for the change may possibly be that Luke
has in mind the position of the martyr before judges who refuse
to debate with him on the truth and falsehood of Christianity
and paganism[4]; Jesus here is the prototype of all martyrs unjustly
condemned by courts which would neither accept the Gospel
nor allow its professors to cross-examine them.

(5) An even more striking instance is the language of the
penitent thief in Lk. 23. 41. His first sentence in v. 40 is quite
poor; κρίμα in the sense of condemnation appears to be peculiar
to biblical Greek; but v. 41 breaks out into fine writing, with
good rhythm καὶ ἡμεῖς μὲν Δικαίως | ἄξια γὰρ ὧν ἐπράξαμεν ἀπολαμβά-
νομεν· | οὗτος Δὲ οὐΔὲν ἄτοπον ἔπραξεν, a contrast with μέν and Δέ, a
cretic with the last long syllables resolved to end the second

---

[1] Cf. *Gentiles*, p. 6, n. 2.

[2] Cf. Norden, *Die ant. Kunstpr.*, p. 486. Note for a similar minor change
Lk. 21. 11, where we have the well-worn assonance of λοιμοὶ καὶ λιμοί as
against Mk. 13. 8.

[3] Creed, ad loc., is inclined to accept the addition of ἢ ἀπολύσητε (AD al
pler latt syrr); but considerations of rhythm are decisive against it. The
addition seems to be due to a scribe who knew nothing of rhythm and was
puzzled by the curious idea of Jesus cross-examining His judges.

[4] The tradition of the hero replying boldly to his judges appears in the
Maccabean tradition; cf. 2 Macc. 6. 24. If, however, Willrich's view (*Ur-
kundenfalschung* in *Forsch. z. Rel. d. a. u. n. T.*, N. F. 21, p. 91 ff.) be accepted,
2 Macc. is later than Caligula's attack on the Temple and little if at all
earlier than the pagan 'martyr-acts' in which Isidorus and his companions
reply with equal boldness to Claudius. For these writings cf. Wilcken, 'Zum
alexand. Antisemitismus', *Abh. d. kön. sächs. Ak. d. Wiss.* (Ph.-Hist. Kl.),
1909, p. 783, and Premerstein, 'Alexandrinische Märtyrerakten', *Philo-
logus*, Supt.-Band 16. 2. 1922, pp. 15 ff. The former notices the resemblance
to the Maccabean language. For the text cf. Pap. Ox. 1. 33. 62 ff. Premerstein, loc. cit. 71 ff., notes the difference between the Christian and pagan
'Acts'.

In Christian literature the boldness of the prisoner before his judges goes
back as far as Act 4. 19, 5. 29, cf. Jno. 18. 34 ff. and below, p. 88, n. 3.

clause, the double assonance of ἄξια, ἐπράξαμεν and ἐπράξαμεν ἀπολαμβάνομεν, and a cretic with both long syllables resolved and a trochee to end clause 3. What follows is, however, lamentable. ' And he said' is the futile ויאמר of the rabbis which does not tell us who the speaker is, and we have the unnecessary σου after βασίλειαν to represent the semitic suffix. The reply of Jesus is equally bad, with its 'and he said to him' which does not tell us who was speaking to whom; it is followed by one of Luke's seven 'Amens'; 'paradise' means in Greek a park, being a loan-word from Persian; it is only in semitic Greek that it means the garden of Eden stored up for the reward of the righteous.[1] The only inference is that Luke had before him a story which puzzled him because of the immense reward promised for so small an act of repentance; he added v. 41 to make the penitence more explicit. The point is of some interest, since it is often held that the Lucan additions to the Passion-narrative represent Luke's working up of his Marcan material; here we have a clear case in which there has been a Lucan addition to or rewriting of material that came to him from a very semitic source. This semitic source of the Passion-narrative used by Luke appears else-where; his story of the prophecy of the betrayal is in a different position from Mark's, 22. 22 (after, not before, the Last Supper). It is also in worse Greek, since Luke has πλήν followed by οὐαὶ where Mark has μὲν . . . 2έ. πλήν as a conjunction is not classical Greek, and while it is frequent in the Gospel, it never appears in the 'we-sections' of Acts. Yet it appears here and in the typically 'Lucan' story of the daughters of Jerusalem; that story too seems to be drawn from an older source.[2]

So far we have dealt with points of style and grammar. In one point Luke's Gospel follows closely the method of hellenistic

---

[1] Cf. Apoc. Moys. 40. 1; 2 En. 8. 1 ff., and Charles's note on 4 Esdr. 8. 52 (*Ap. and Ps.* 2. 597); 2 Co. 12. 4. The eschatology implied is that of the parable of Dives and Lazarus. Cf. Creed on Lk. 16. 23.

[2] In the Gospel πλήν as a rather strong 'but' is used 15 times (or 13 if 17. 1 and 22. 42 be rejected with Tischendorf and WH marg. as due to assimilation with Mt.). In Acts it is never used in this sense, πλήν ὅτι in 20. 23 being classical (cf. Blass, *Gr. N.T. Gr.* 268). It is rare in other N.T. writers (Mt. 5 times, St. Paul 3 times with πλὴν ὅτι once in Phil. 1. 18; also in Eph. 5. 33). In itself the use is good koine (LSJ. quote Polybius 1. 69. 14). It is scarcely credible that its frequency in Luke should be due to himself since he never uses it in Acts. It seems to have been used in Q (e.g. Mt. 11. 22 and 24 = Lk. 10. 11 and 14), but Mt. tends to change it, or uses a slightly different version in which it was not used. Luke has no objection to it, but he does not use it when writing himself.

literature. Mark represents Jesus as a travelling teacher; it is quite probable that this came to him from older tradition. But Luke expands the Marcan journeys. He had a large block of material not found elsewhere. He also had in Mk. 10. 32 the beginning of a journey from Galilee to Jerusalem and in Mk. 10. 46 Jesus' arrival at Jericho. Luke simply dresses his extra material up as a travel-story and inserts it into the Marcan journey, without noticing the impossibility that a journey which passed through Samaria in 9. 52 should be passing through Jericho in 18. 35, thus making his narrative conform to the pattern of hellenistic literature, in which the story of the travelling teacher or wonder-worker was a favourite theme.[1]

Here he had before him the Marcan tradition as a justification. In Acts he had no doubt an even greater justification, since it is not open to doubt that St. Paul's journeys covered the ground which the narrative of Acts describes. But the fact that his story is based on a hellenistic pattern in which the journeys of the hero are simply a framework, into which are fitted specimen incidents of teaching and wonder-working, means that it is sheer waste of ink to discuss the real or apparent discrepancies between the narrative of Acts and the movements between Athens and Thessalonica implied in 1 Thess. 3. 1 ff., or between Antioch and Jerusalem as implied in Gal. 2[2]; it is equally irrelevant to ask why he has omitted St. Paul's journeys between Ephesus and Corinth implied in 2 Cor. 12. 14 ff. The journeys are a mere framework, and were never intended as a detailed itinerary. Even the shipwreck which forms the climax of Acts is a regular theme of hellenistic writing. No doubt the story is true; but the elaborate description just at the climax of the story seems to be inspired by the general convention; the earlier shipwrecks referred to in 2 Cor. 11. 25, one of which was a far more serious affair, are not even mentioned.[3]

[1] Cf. Creed, op. cit. 140: 'The explanation of the geographical journey is therefore literary.'

[2] Cf. Norden, *Agnostos Theos*, 34 ff.; Rohde, *Die griechische Roman*[2], 327, who quotes instances going back to Diogenes. Such journeys were often made to undertake an ἐπίδειξις at a great festival; for the theme in the Fourth Gospel cf. below, p. 68, n. 2. For the supposed discrepancies cf. Lake, *Earlier Epistles of St. Paul*, 73 ff.; Cadbury, *Beginnings*, 4, 224 ff. for 1 Thess. 3. 1 ff.; and for Acts 15 and Gal. 2 cf. Windisch, *Beginnings*, 2. 317 ff.; I cannot allow that there is any discrepancy here, cf. *Jerusalem*, 219 ff.

[3] For the shipwreck theme cf. Dio Chrys. 7. 2 f., v. Arn. 1. 190; Aristides, Ἱεροὶ Λόγοι 2. 65 ff. (Keil, 2. 409); Ach. Tat. Leuc. et Clit. 3. 1 ff. Wendland,

To turn to the Acts as a whole, the first half of the book is quite largely written in more or less translation Greek[1]; the second half falls into two strata, the travel-diary and the account of Paul's journeys where Luke himself was not an eyewitness. The general level of the Greek in these two strata is far higher, and there seems no reason for supposing that we are not dealing with Luke's own diary and St. Paul's reminiscences, as edited by him. It is interesting, however, to notice that Luke's liking for a piece of good rhetorical prose betrays itself occasionally in the first part of the book. A notable instance is St. Stephen's speech, a peculiar document, possibly from a very early Christian source,[2] containing a kerygma of the history of Israel constructed so as to prove that the Jews have always been in error.[3] As a whole the speech is an atrocity of semitic Greek, filled with O.T. quotations and barbarous names.[4] But in v. 43 we have an apparently pointless alteration of Amos 5. 27 ' I will carry you away beyond Damascus' into 'I will carry you away beyond Babylon'. Various attempts have been made to explain the alteration.[5] But the effect of the alteration is that this section of the speech is made to end not, as Amos does in the LXX with the worst possible rhetorical ending, the end of a hexameter (ἐπέκεινα Δαμάσκου), but with the best possible; for

Hell.-röm. Kultur, 2. 324, ascribes Acts 27. 9 ff., to a supposed final redactor, objecting to St. Paul's supposed foreknowledge of the wreck. Aristides, loc. cit. 67, claims to have given a similar warning which was ignored with equally disastrous results. Professional mariners would always be likely to take risks which the passengers deprecated; the passengers when disaster happened could hardly resist the temptation to say 'I told you so'.

Windisch in *Beginnings*, 2. 304, notes various attempts to treat the whole travel-story as fiction, on the ground that similar passages in the first person are found in purely fictitious narratives. But for the method of writing cf. Norden, *Agnostos Theos*, 316 ff., who notes parallels from Velleius Paterculus and Ammianus Marcellinus as well as from the Alexander-romances. The parallels also show that Windisch's objection to the suddenness with which the first person is introduced is unfounded and does not imply clumsy compilation by an editor who is not the author of the 'we-sections'. On this cf. Meyer, *Urspr. u. Anf.* 3. 19 ff.

[1] Cf. Torrey, *Composition and Date of Acts* (*Harvard Theological Studies*, 1) and De Zwaan's criticism of Torrey in *Beginnings*, 2. 30 ff., especially the latter's recognition of the effect of the LXX and books of Testimonies, as well as of the growing 'Christian Greek' of the Church even on writers of good Greek. He recognizes only 1. 1*b*–5. 16 and 9. 31–11. 18 as necessarily involving a 'translation-Greek' source.

[2] Cf. Meyer, *Urspr. u. Anf.* 3. 158 ff.   [3] Cf. *Jerusalem*, 43.

[4] Norden, *Ant. Kunstpr.* 484 ff.

[5] Cf. Foakes Jackson in Moffatt's *Commentary*, ad loc.

ἐπέκεινα Βαβυλῶνος gives a cretic with the second long syllable resolved and a trochee, the famous *esse videatur* of Cicero; I suspect that Luke merely wanted to substitute rhythm for a metrical jingle, and had no deep theological motives. The dramatic ending of the speech need not of course be ascribed to Luke's source, if he has simply incorporated an earlier document. There is every reason to suppose that he wrote it himself. It is amazingly successful as a denunciation by an angry man fighting desperately for his life. The effect is produced by heaping up the 'harsh' consonants of rhetorical tradition; on a normal average we should find κ, π, τ, and ξ about 36 times in a passage of this length, but in the closing paragraph we find them 52 times[1]; in the last sentence a string of short syllables, again regarded as harsh in rhetoric, leads up to the intolerable καὶ οὐκ ἐφυλάξατε with 4 harsh consonants in 6, and 5 syllables out of 6 short (καὶ οὐκ being run together).[2] It must be remembered that an elementary knowledge of rhetoric was almost universal among the public for which Luke was writing, the partially educated Graeco-Roman world.[3] There is an

---

[1] For the Greek view of the harshness of these consonants and of naturally (not metrically) short as against long vowels cf. Dion Halic. De Compositione Verborum, 14, embodying the conventional rhetorical tradition. A comparison of this passage with others chosen at random from speeches in Acts of approximately the same length gives the following results:

	κ	π	τ	ξ	Total
Acts 7. 51–6	12	11	27	2	52
4. 9–12 (οἰκοδόμων) . .	5	6	20	1	32
7. 37–9 (ἀπώσαντο) . .	6	6	22	1	35
13. 31–3 (Δευτέρῳ) . .	6	10	20	0	36
17. 22–4	10	10	19	0	39
17. 25–7	10	12	20	1	43
22. 14 (θεός)–17 (Ἰερουσαλήμ)	9	8	22	0	39
24. 2–5 (Ἰουδαίοις) . .	8	10	23	1	42
24. 10–12	6	11	15	0	32
24. 18–21	7	9	20	1	37
26. 2–4	6	8	14	0	28

The small number in the last passage is especially noticeable, since it is a carefully worded compliment to Agrippa.

[2] Contrast the effect which would have been secured by the excellent rhetorical ending οἵτινες ἠθετήσατε τὸν νόμον τὸν δοθέντα εἰς διαταγὰς ἀγγέλων (double cretic with the first long syllable resolved).

[3] Cf. Tacitus, Dial. 19 'pervulgatis iam omnibus, cum vix in cortina quisquam adsistat, quin elementis studiorum, etsi non instructus, at certe imbutus sit'. Compare the opening sentence of the speech, where ἄνδρες ἀδελφοί is followed by a string of short syllables leading up to the harsh ὁ θεὸς τῆς δόξης found in Ps. 29. 3, but not particularly common or appropriate here. The trick is

equally striking effect in 23.1–3, where St. Paul defends himself
as a good Jew; his opening words have 18 long vowels and the
harsh consonants are avoided (κ 0, π 3, τ 5, ξ 0). But when the
High Priest orders the bystanders to strike him on the mouth
St. Paul loses his temper and we have only 15 long vowels out
of 40 (allowing τύπτειν to be naturally short), and 17 harsh
consonants (κ 7, π 3, τ 7). It is perhaps remarkable that in this
sudden outburst of anger St. Paul should remember his rhetoric
well enough to introduce the chiasmus with antithesis involved
in κάθη κρίνων με κατὰ τὸν νόμον καὶ παρανομῶν κελεύεις με τύπτεσθαι.

(3) We have a very peculiar Lucan improvement in 8. 31.
Here Philip meets the Ethiopian eunuch reading his Bible; the
passage as a whole is marked by a thoroughly semitic use of
parataxis and a lack of particles except the inevitable καὶ
occasionally varied by δέ. Into this episode Luke inserts a little
gem of Greek conversation, in which Philip opens with ἆρά γε
followed by the play on the words γινώσκεις ἃ ἀναγινώσκεις and
the eunuch replies with the almost obsolete ἄν with the optative.[1]
What the history lying behind the incident may be is not very
easy to decide; the pious Ethiopian might be drawn from
Zephaniah 3.10,[2] but it was a commonplace of hellenistic literature that the Ethiopians, living at the back of beyond, were an
exceptionally pious race.[3] It is at least possible that the story
goes back to some visionary experience of Philip, as the vague-
ness of the account may perhaps indicate. Luke would appear
to have used the story as an excuse for bringing in one of the
main O.T. testimonies to Christianity, that of Isaiah 53. 7 f., at
this point, introducing it by the remarkable dialogue between
Philip and the barbarian.

This incident is typical of Luke's method of dealing with his
precisely that of Cicero's 'Quousque tandem abutere, Catilina, patientia
nostra' (In Cat. 1. 1).

[1] Cf. Blass, Gr. N.T. Greek, 220, for Luke's use of literary rather than popular language in this matter. For καὶ ἰδού in v. 27 see below, p. 17, n. 2. The
omission of the article before πνεῦμα κυρίου in v. 39 is probably also due to
semitic influence; contrast τὸ πνεῦμα 'Ιησοῦ in 16. 7.

[2] Cf. Lowther Clarke in Beginnings, 2. 101, and note that in Zeph. 2. 4
'Gaza shall be forsaken and Ashdod a wilderness'.

[3] Diod. Sic. 3. 2. 2 ff.; Philostratus, Vita Apoll. Tyan. 6. 2; Pausanias,
1. 33. 5; Nic. Damasc. fr. 142 (F.G.H. (Jacoby) 2. 385); cf. Erman, Die Rel.
der Aegypter, 355. For the popularity of the theme of the pious barbarians
living in some remote region cf. Rohde, Die gr. Rom.[2] 210 ff. (they can even
be removed to China) and for the Ethiopians in particular, p. 470. For the
real state of Ethiopia at the period cf. Strabo, Geogr. 17. 1. 54 (820) ff.,
following good Roman information.

sources. In general he reproduces them faithfully with minor improvements of style,[1] though his methods of revision are so spasmodic that as in the Gospel he preserves language which he avoids in his own writing.[2] The speeches in Acts are no doubt Luke's own composition in so far as they represent what he thought appropriate to the particular character on the particular occasion; but apart from the speech of St. Stephen, where he may incorporate a written source, it would seem that the speeches for the most part follow a conventional pattern of preaching, which probably corresponds in general to the method actually used. Otherwise it is impossible to say how far the speeches record genuine reminiscences of St. Paul's own words where Luke may have heard them. It must, however, be noted to his credit that he has made no attempt to glorify his hero by representing him as a cultivated orator;[3] his speech at Antioch abounds in barbarisms.[4] His speech before Agrippa has a reasonably good opening and an apology for the use of the name 'Saul' in the 'Hebrew tongue'. It is quite probable that here he is faithful to St. Paul's practice, if not to his words; a good opening, breaking down as the speaker warmed to his work, is what we should expect from the Pauline Epistles. So much for

[1] A specimen to which no importance attaches is Lk. 23. 56—24. 1, where he has rewritten Mk. 15. 47. He has inserted μέν . . . δέ and the classical ὄρθρου.

[2] Cf. above, p. 8 and p. 12, n. 7. Another instance is the semitic καὶ ἰδού which has penetrated into the koine and is frequent in Luke except in the 'we-sections' where it appears only in 20. 22 and 25, and 27. 24, all reported Pauline speeches. Note that it appears in 16. 1, where it seems pointless, and not in 16. 9, which clamours for it. The reason seems to be that 16. 1 goes back to Pauline reminiscences embodying recollections of the early controversies when it was important to insist that Timothy had been circumcised and to explain the reason. On the other hand, 16. 9 does not use the phrase because we are dealing with Luke's own diary, which avoids it.

[3] The town clerk at Ephesus speaks excellent Greek, as does Tertullus (Acts 19. 35 ff. and 24. 2 ff.; see Note II to this Lecture).

[4] Acts 13. 16 ff.; note particularly vv. 21–3 with 6 barbarian names. On the other hand, the introduction of the whole theology of grace and the Law in 13. 38 is clearly unhistorical. St. Paul would never have relegated it to a subordinate position in this way. Luke introduces it here in order to summarize Paul's Gospel; his knowledge that the Jews will reject it reflects the later history of the Pauline missions and perhaps earlier and unrecorded incidents in Syria and Cilicia. For the ancient practice of summarizing a long process in a single specimen incident cf. Meyer, *Gesch. d. Alt.*[2] 1. 218 f. (The allusion to Saul might be a genuine reminiscence: was it a synagogue practice to glorify your eponymous hero in the O.T.? Cf. the glorification of Eliezer, Abraham's servant, by R. Eliezer in Talmud Yôma 28 b.)

D

the Acts; so far as I can see he has followed his sources here as in the Gospel with remarkable fidelity except for occasional verbal improvements, using only the normal licence with regard to his speeches.

It has been said that Luke is unduly fond of the miraculous,[1] but the charge cannot really be maintained. Apart from the central miracle his infancy narrative is far less miraculous than Matthew's.[2] Nor does the rest of the Gospel support the charge. We find a miraculous draught of fishes at the call of St. Peter; but the story is told in language which is certainly not Luke's but that of a source very little removed from the Aramaic tradition. The same applies to the story of the rejection of Nazareth sometimes quoted as an instance of this tendency. It is probable that Luke has transferred it to the opening of the ministry as dramatically appropriate. But he has not invented the extended form of the discourse of Jesus, as the word ἀμήν shows. And there is no reason to suppose that the words 'Jesus going through the midst of them went His way' imply a miracle; the only thing to do with an angry crowd is to walk straight through it.[3] The only miracle which he can be suspected of having added to the tradition he received in the Gospel is the healing of the ear of the High Priest's servant in 22. 51. In the 'we-sections' of Acts the miraculous element is notably diminished, even if we include in them the story of the escape of Paul and Silas at Philippi[4] which does not actually fall into the 'we-sections'; since the writer of these sections is at Philippi in 16. 16

[1] Streeter, *The Four Gospels*, 220.

[2] For the text of Lk. 1. 34 where the variant text of b has been taken as evidence that Luke did not originally record a miraculous birth cf. Creed, ad loc.

[3] For the incident cf. Creed, 65 ff. But there is no evidence that a miraculous escape is intended. In any case, the story comes from a source which knows that death by stoning took the form of precipitation from a height (Mishnah Sanh. 6. 4, Tos. Sanh. 9. 6 a). Elsewhere Luke implies that it took the form of pelting with stones, as it originally did (Josh. 7. 25, Lev. 24. 14), by his use of λιθοβολεῖν (Acts 7. 58, 14. 5). λιθάζειν in Acts 14. 19, 2 Cor. 11. 25 presumably means the same (cf. Jno. 10. 31). It seems that Luke is following a source which knew the Mishnaic procedure, though Luke himself does not realize it. Presumably the other form was common enough in riots.

[4] The whole section 16. 25–35 could be eliminated as the work of a final editor, but the linguistic evidence is against the attempt. μεσονύκτιον is a poetical Ionic word found in good koine; the story is told in good periods like the rest of this part of Acts (cf. de Zwaan, *Beginnings*, 2. 33). Escapes from prison are, of course, a frequent theme of this kind of literature; Cadbury, *Beginnings*, 4. 196 f., gives numerous parallels. Singing is a frequent

and reappears there in 20.5 he would seem to have spent the whole intervening period in the city, and must in any case have been able to ascertain the history of the Church there. It seems probable that he has accepted a legend which had grown up round a remarkable escape of some kind, and had acquired a certain accretion of pious embroidery of a conventional type; but this is merely to say that he believed in the miraculous, as did anyone who was not a conscientious Epicurean. The only other miracles recorded in the 'we-sections' are the raising of Eutychus, where it is by no means clear that a miracle is intended,[1] the incident of the serpent at Malta,[2] where again it is not certain that a miracle is intended, and the healing of the son of Publius at Malta, a miracle of a type which must have been frequent in the early Christian missions.[3] In view of the general atmosphere of N. T. Christianity, this is a very small allowance of the miraculous element. It is even possible to hold that in his Gospel he has modified the Marcan miracle of the cursing of the barren fig-tree into a parable, though it is more probable that the parable was the original, in view of its derivation from a piece of popular folk-lore of a kind which Jesus may well have used for a parable.[4] Thus there seems no reason to suppose that

feature of such stories (Cadbury, loc. cit.; to his parallels add Test. Jos. 8 quoted by de Zwaan, op. cit. 2. 78). But as Cadbury notes it is certain that Paul and Silas would have been singing in such circumstances: granting the fact of the escape the rest of the story would grow up inevitably. The baptism of the jailer with no preliminary instruction is in favour of a very early date; the catechumenate seems to be established in Heb. 6. 1 ff.; it is well established by the time of the Apostolic Tradition of Hippolytus (dated by Easton, p. 86 of his edition, to the first century A.D.). Justin Martyr, Apol. 1. 61 (93 d), implies a course of preliminary instruction. The Acts of Paul and Thecla (25) represents St. Paul as refusing to baptize Thecla without a proper catechumenate, so that she has to baptize herself (ib. 34); James (Apocr. N.T. 270) dates this work about A.D. 160. See also Note, p. 95.

For the reduction of the miraculous element in these sections cf. Meyer, Urspr. u. Anf. 3. 16 and 27 ff.

[1] Cf. Cadbury's note ad loc.; Beginnings, 4. 256.

[2] Cadbury, Beginnings, 4. 341 insists that καθῆψεν must mean 'bit' but Voc. Gr. N.T., s. voc. ἔχιδνα, gives 'fastened on'.

[3] Cf. 1 Cor. 12. 28, Gal. 3. 5, where St. Paul's argument would be meaningless if his opponents could answer by denying that any mighty works had happened.

[4] Creed, ad loc., seems to imply that Luke has changed the miracle of Mark into a parable; Streeter, The Four Gospels, 178, treats the parable as the original. Smith (Parables of the Synoptic Gospels, 63) points out the resemblance to the story of Ahikar, 8. 35. But the story is drawn from the popular magic recipe ascribed to 'Zoroaster' (Geoponica, 10. 83), drawn apparently from the pseudo-Zoroastrian περὶ φύσεως going back to about

Luke has added seriously to the miraculous element in the Gospel.[1] In any case we need not regard credulity as a hellenistic characteristic; in so far as the hellenistic age witnessed a growth of credulity it was due not to the influence of Greece on the East but to the influence on Greece of oriental religions, among which Judaism was pre-eminent in its fondness for edifying miracles. Luke has endeavoured to impose a certain improvement of style on his very intractable material; but he has done so with a remarkable lack of consistency.[2] He has made a few additions to relate the Gospel to world-history, as in his chronological introduction, and he has made some insertions to explain away difficulties in his sources, or for purposes of edification.[3] There are a few changes introduced to meet the growing tendency to Gnosticism in the primitive Church.[4] In Acts he has not

250 B.C. (Cumont and Bidez, *Les Mages hellénisés*, 1. 109 ff. and 120 ff.). It is a piece of popular magic which may or may not have a Persian or Babylonian origin. The owner of a barren tree should gird up his loins and go up to the tree in anger as if to cut it down. Someone else must come up and ask him to spare the tree, guaranteeing that it will do better in future; if spared, the tree will bear well. It looks as though the parable is intended as an allusion to popular superstitions which the hearers would understand. For a similar case in which a parable may have become an incident cf. Smith, op. cit. 67, where it is suggested that the story of the Widow's mite was originally a parable. (He rightly rejects the theory of Buddhist influence; to the parallels from rabbinical literature which he quotes should be added the collection of stories in Porphyry περὶ ἀποχῆς 2. 15 ff. from Theophrastus, De Pietate, and Theopompus.)

[1] For the Widow's son at Nain cf. above, p. 1. His resurrection story is a good specimen of his methods. The narrative is in very semitic Greek; for καὶ ἰδοῦ in 24. 13, cf. p. 17, n. 2. The usage ἦσαν πορευόμενοι in 24. 13, cf. 32, is common in Luke–Acts up to Acts 13, but rare and with special reasons later; cf. Blass, op. cit. 204, for this as an Aramaism. There is at times an extravagant use of the semitic pronoun (13 ff., 30 f., 36, 50 ff.). But the dialogue is good; it appears to be a typical kerygma in process of development. Jesus has been crucified and proves that His death and resurrection are κατὰ τὰς γραφάς. Creed also comments ad loc. on the lack of a reference to the Parousia. It looks as though Luke had added the dialogue to a story which reached him from a semitic source.

[2] De Zwaan in *H.T.R.* 17. 2. 95 ff. (April 1924) argues from the irregularities of the style that Acts was a posthumous edition; but his argument, though interesting, fails to allow for similar phenomena in the Gospel. Many of these have been noted already. Note also that the Good Samaritan appears to have undergone a linguistic revision (cf. Creed on Lk. 10. 25). But in the parable of the Great Supper his version seems more primitive than Matthew's (cf. Smith, op. cit. 205) and the Greek is more semitic (note the parataxis in the excuses in 14. 18 ff., as contrasted with Mt. 22. 5).

[3] Cf. above, pp. 11 f.

[4] Cf. *Gentiles*, 149, n. 5, and add the semi-Gnostic interpretation of the

given us as full an account as we could wish of the controversies of the primitive Church; but here he is simply following the general method of describing a lengthy process in a selected episode. In general the licence which he allows himself in dealing with his sources does not go beyond the view of great historians of antiquity that it is the function of history to convey ethical and political instruction.[1]

On the other hand, Luke is a true hellenist in the sense that he has really grasped the fact that if history is to give instruction of this kind it must be true history; it must be a narrative of events which actually occurred, not of events which ought to have occurred in order to support the writer's thesis. Such a view was entirely alien to the Jewish mind, which was so concerned to interpret history in the light of the divine purpose which was assumed to underlie it, that it was content to falsify the facts indefinitely in the interests of edification.[2] The Marcan account of the life of Jesus was already a theological account in which Jesus was the Son of God; we can see occasional traces of the growth of pious legend around the solid core of oral traditions.[3] The natural course of development is represented by Matthew's tendency to transform history into legend in order to represent the life of Jesus as the fulfilment of prophecy, or on the other hand by the Fourth Gospel, for which factual truth is

parable of the sower by the Elders in Ir. Haer. 5. 36. 2, cf. Clem. Alex. Strom. 6. 14. 114 (798 P.); Orig. In Luc. Fr. lxxix. 24. Luke's omission of the Marcan cry from the Cross may be due to similar motives, cf. the Gospel of Peter, Akhmin Fr. 19, *Apocr. N.T.* 91, Ir. Haer. 1. 1. 16 and 1.21. 1. Dibelius ascribes the omission and the alteration in the Gospel of Peter to dogmatic motives, ignoring the meaning of δύναμις here, for which cf. *Gentiles*, 115 (*From Tradition to Gospel*, 194). The omission of Lk. 22. 43 in some MSS. appears to be due to reverential omission rather than to antidocetic insertion, which would hardly go so far (cf. Streeter, op. cit. 61, against Creed, ad loc.). If 22. 43 be genuine, Luke would hardly have objected to the cry from the Cross on reverential grounds. But he may simply have objected to it as a barbarism in its Aramaic form; or it may be simply due to clumsy scissors-and-paste work in conflating his sources.

[1] Thuc. 1. 22, Polyb. 1. 1. 2 who excuses himself from discussing the point at length on the ground that it is generally recognized.

[2] The best instance of this is the Chronicler's method of explaining either the misfortunes of good kings or the prosperity of bad ones; note, e.g., the insertion of 2 Chron. 24. 15 ff. on Joash; 25. 14 (Amaziah); 26. 16 ff. (Uzziah); 30. 1 ff. (Hezekiah's Passover); 33. 11 ff. (Manasseh's captivity in Babylon and his subsequent repentance, to explain the fact that he died in his bed).

[3] Cf. Hoskyns and Davey, *Riddle of the N.T.*, for an exposition of the theological tendencies underlying this Gospel, at times elaborated to a somewhat fanciful extent.

entirely subordinated to doctrinal interpretation. The final stage is represented by the complete detachment of the Gnostic Gospels from historical truth. It is largely due to the hellenic interest in historical truth as such, manifested by St. Luke in associating the Gospel tradition, which he accepted as he received it, with the history of the early Christian missions as he knew them at first hand, that Christianity remains a religion rooted in history.

NOTE I

The Infancy Narratives of the N.T.

The accounts of the virgin birth of Jesus are sometimes classed with the legends of primitive folk-lore; this is as ludicrous as to class the supposedly miraculous births of Plato, Alexander, and Augustus with such legends; the only connexion between the primitive belief and the later stories, if any, is that the primitive legends in some cases survived in folk-lore and mythology and so led to a belief that a miraculous birth was in some way suitable for anyone whose greatness made him the equal of the heroes of antiquity.

Greek mythology abounds in such stories (for a full list of real or imagined parallels cf. Clemen, *Religionsgesch. Erkl. d. N.T.*[2] 192 ff.). Jewish mythology in its O.T. form has none. The mythology of Ras Shamra (cf. Dussaud, *Découvertes de Ras Shamra*, 81 ff.) contains a story of the birth of the gods associated with a sacred marriage, which suggests that primitive semitic folk-lore may have contained stories of this kind. In any case, whether as a result of its contact with other civilizations or as a result of the survival in popular folk-lore of a mythology which has been eliminated from the O.T., Judaism about the beginning of the Christian era abounded in stories of miraculous births.

(1) Noah. The O.T. suggests no ground for an infancy narrative, but 1 Enoch 106. 2 ff. describes him as being born with a body whiter than snow and redder than a rose, his hair white as wool (cf. Dan. 7. 9); when he opened his mouth the house shone (Zoroaster's birth has a similar portent, cf. below, p. 25, n. 1). Noah here is a quasi-Messianic figure; Charles, *Ap. and Ps.* 2. 168, dates the Noachic parts of 1 En. before the Book of Jubilees; 1 Enoch 6–11 from the same stratum in the Book of Enoch appears to contain pre-biblical traditions (cf. Cook, *The Old Testament, a Reinterpretation*, 36 ff.)

(2) Abraham. For the astral portents which accompanied his birth cf. Str.-B. on Mt. 2. 2; for Nimrod's attempt to destroy him and his concealment by his parents cf. Pirke de R. Eliezer, 31a. ii.

(3) The story of Isaac offered abundant scope for rabbinical enlargements on the miraculous character of his birth in view of his parents' old age (Gen. 17. 17 and 18. 11). On these passages cf. Gen. R. ad loc. (ed. Theodor 472 and 493), Yalkut 78 (Warsaw ed. 1876, p. 43b).

Here we have a miraculous rejuvenation of his parents. It is to be noted that Porphyry, quoted by Eusebius Pr. Ev. 1. 10. 30 (= 4. 16. 7), has a remarkable version of the story of Isaac's sacrifice in Gen. 22 taken from Philo of Byblos, who presumably derived it from Sanchuniathon. Sanchuniathon appears to have offered his euhemeristic version of Phoenician mythology (Eus. Pr. Ev. 1. 10. 23) in opposition to the older exposition in terms of allegory and physical speculation of Thabion (ib. 20), who is dated by Dussaud (op. cit. 72) to the fourteenth century B.C. (For other features of biblical mythology in these texts cf. Dussaud, op. cit. 83 ff., 101 ff., and especially 111 ff. for the story of Gen. 15.) The story describes the sacrifice by Cronos, whom the Phoenicians call Israel, of his only son, 'Ιεούδ (יחיד), whose mother was a nymph called Anobret; but the circumstances of the sacrifice are those of the king of Moab's sacrifice of his son in 2 Kings 3. 27, a story which is practically contemporary with the story of Gen. 22 in its present form (cf. Ryle in Hastings, D.B. 2. 145 ff., who holds the story to be of Ephraimite origin and drawn from E, with Moriah substituted for an Ephraimite sanctuary, and Woods ib. 2. 373, who dates the story slightly before Amos and Hosea). Thus it is at least possible that Eusebius has preserved a version of the story older than that of Gen. 22 and far less edifying; it is also to be noted that Bochart, quoted by Heinichen on Eus. Pr. Ev. 1. 10. 30, suggests that 'Anobret' = חן עוברת 'she who conceived by grace'. It seems that the original story of Isaac goes back to polytheistic mythology; it is conceivable that his wonderful birth was known in popular folk-lore as well as in the embroideries of rabbinical exegesis.

(4) Moses' birth in the O.T. is quite natural and unconnected with the decision of Pharaoh to exterminate the Hebrews. But Josephus, Antt. 2. 205, gives a whole cycle of legends. Pharaoh's decision was due to a prophecy that a child was to be born who 'would humble the empire of Egypt and exalt the Israelites'; Amram after his birth was told by God in a dream that he would deliver Israel; Moses refused to be suckled by any but a Jewess; when Pharaoh put his crown on Moses' head, he dashed it to the ground, an omen of the future. In Philo, De Vit. Moys. 1. 19, Pharaoh's daughter pretends that he is her son, and Moses makes miraculous progress in his education; the edifying detail that he preferred the deliverance of Israel to the crown of Egypt (Philo, op. cit. 32 and Heb. 11. 25) can be read into Exodus, but does not appear there. For rabbinical versions of the legends cf. Str.-B. on Mt. 2. 16. Josephus' story goes back to the propaganda of Alexandrine Judaism, fragments of which, combined with the anti-semitic propaganda of Manetho (cf. Jos. c. Ap. 1. 238 ff.), appear in Strabo 16. 2. 35 (760) and Diod. Sic. 40. 3. 3. It would be interesting to know if this Jewish propaganda was based entirely on the O.T. and the inventive faculties of the pseudo-Hecataeus, or whether it preserved any popular legends; it may be observed that the story was originally non-Jewish, cf.

Meyer, *Die Isr. u. ihre Nachbarstämme*, 46 ff.) and that Hall, *Ancient History of the Near East*, 408, suggests that Manetho's identification of Moses with the runaway Egyptian priest Osarsiph may imply his knowledge of an Egyptian legend out of which the Moses story in the O.T. has been developed; if so, it is possible that some of Josephus' legends of Moses' birth were drawn from Jewish or Egyptian folk-lore. In any case the story of the exposure and finding of Moses in Exodus would be natural in the legend of a child of divine parentage and would easily be interpreted as implying the favourite *motif* of a massacre of the Innocents. (For this cf. Suet. Aug. 94. 3; Julius Marathus, the freedman of Augustus, recorded a prophecy of his future and a consequent decision of the Senate to massacre all children born that year; it would be interesting to know whether Julius Marathus was of Syrian or Egyptian origin.)

(5) In the case of Samuel we have a remarkable birth attached to a great sanctuary; for this cf. Frazer, *Folk-lore in the O.T.*, who suggests that the story originally included a divine paternity.

(6) Samson's birth is again attended by miraculous phenomena; it may be noted that Judges 13 appears to be derived from J, while his exploits are drawn from solar mythology and popular folk-lore. It is at least possible that there was originally a less edifying introduction, which the present c. 13 has replaced. (Cf. Burney, *The Book of Judges*, 335 ff.)

Thus the *motif* of a miraculous birth was in no way strange to Jewish thought. We find a belief in miraculous birth from a virgin very near Jewish soil in Epiphanius' account of the annual festival held at Petra, the Nabatean capital, on 6. Jan. (Panar. 51. 22; for Dusares cf. Bousset, *Kyrios Christos*[2], 270 ff.; Clemen, *Religionsgesch. Erkl. d. N.T.*[2], 118 ff.; Robertson-Smith, *Religion of the Semites*[3], 56, and Cook's note on p. 520). A similar festival is recorded at Elusa near Gaza (Epiphanius loc. cit.; for this festival and its relation to the Aeon-festival at Alexandria cf. Cumont, *Comptes Rendus de l'Acad. d. Inscr.* 1911, 292 ff.). Here the festival was definitely solar; it was held on 25 Dec., and part of the rite was the cry 'The Virgin hath born a son, the light increases'. For these festivals and their possible connexion with the O.T. stories and the birth-prophecy of Is. 7. 14, cf. Kittel, *Die hell. Myst.-rel. u. d. a. T.* (Beitr. z. Wiss. v. a. T., n. F. 7).

In any case, these festivals seem to stand much nearer to the beliefs of popular Judaism than the Alexandrine festival of Kore and Aion on 6 Jan. [Professor Nock in 'A vision of Mandulis-Aion', *H.T.R.* 27. 1. 93 ff. (Jan. 1934) suggests that here the date, the solar significance, and the name of Aion have been grafted on to an older feast with Eleusinian affinities]. If they are really ancient Nabatean festivals, they would appear to have a solar character. Dusares indeed is identified with Dionysus, but the identification is not, it would appear, ancient, the vine having been unknown to the Nabateans before the Hellenistic era (Robertson-Smith, op. cit. 193); as the יחיד of Baal he could easily be the sun (Bousset, loc. cit., treats the title given him by Epiphanius μονογενής τοῦ λεσπότου as if it had some significance for Christian origins, but it is simply a literal translation of the semitic title for Dusares as a solar deity; cf. P.W.K. v. 2. 1867). It is at least possible that the birth of Samson in the O.T. replaces a miraculous birth of a solar deity in ancient semitic religion, and that legends with regard to it survived into the N.T. period. It would seem far more probable that the story of the virgin birth has been influenced by such popular folk-lore than by the Alexandrine festival, or again by Philo, De Cher. 43 ff. (For the attempt of Norden in *Die Geburt d. Kindes* to derive the story from this source cf. the admirable discussion by Creed in *The Gospel according to St. Luke*, 15.) On the other hand, it is perfectly possible that the story was derived from the rabbinical exaggerations of the story of the birth of Isaac.

Naturally if the story of the virgin birth be accepted as historically true, the question of the source or sources of the idea does not arise. On the other hand, it is naturally tempting for those who reject it to regard it as a 'hellenistic' accretion which was no part of the original Gospel. But there is no evidence that the narratives in the N.T. are 'hellenistic' in the sense that they could not have been derived from purely Jewish ideas and beliefs. It is true that we have no evidence of other stories of a virgin birth in Jewish literature; but the same applies to Greek beliefs in miraculous births, where we have not a virgin birth but a divine paternity.[1]

NOTE II

The Speeches in Acts

The speeches in Acts are discussed by Cadbury in *Beginnings*, 5. 402 ff.; to the literature quoted there should be added Dodd's study of the subject in *The Apostolic Preaching and its Developments*. Cadbury's conclusions in general are clearly right; this note is intended to deal with a few difficulties in certain speeches and a few points in which they throw a certain light on Luke's methods.

(1) Acts 5. 34 ff. We have a notorious difficulty, since Paul claims that he was educated at the feet of Gamaliel (Acts 22. 3) and ought to

[1] It may be noted that we also have a story of the miraculous birth of Zoroaster, for which cf. Jackson, *Zoroaster the Prophet of Ancient Iran*, 24 ff. His birth was surrounded by portents, including the appearance of a star which shone round the house where he was born (cf. *Protev. Jac.* 19. 2; James, *Apocr. N.T.* 46). His enemies attempted to kill him, though there is no story of a massacre of the Innocents. He laughed at his birth, a story known to Pliny (N.H. 7. 72). It would of course be possible to trace the hellenistic and Jewish beliefs in miraculous births to Persian sources, but it seems far more probable that the various stories are independent expressions of the belief that the great figures of history ought to have a more than human origin.

have known what he said or might have said on the occasion, but the speech contains an historical blunder. Judas of Galilee rebelled in A.D. 6 or 7 while the rising of Theudas occurred when Fadus was procurator after the death of Herod Agrippa I in A.D. 44 (cf. Schürer, *G.J.V.* 1. 486 and 566). Josephus, Antt. 20. 97 and 102, describes a rising of the grandsons of Judas shortly after the rising of Theudas and it has been held that Luke has read Josephus carelessly. So late a date for Acts is, however, difficult; Streeter (*The Four Gospels*, 557) suggests that he may have heard Josephus lecture in Rome; it is perhaps as likely that both are drawing on a common source which Luke has copied inaccurately. But I am inclined to suspect that Luke reflects a Palestinian source which emphasized the real or supposed coincidence between the birth of Jesus and the beginning of 'false Christs' with Judas of Galilee (cf. above, p. 10, n. 1); he had also heard of Theudas, but knew little about his date. It should be observed that both Theudas and 'the Egyptian' of Acts 21. 38 and Antt. 20. 169 promise to work miracles modelled on these of Joshua (3. 14 ff. and 6. 20). It is at least possible that they claimed to be Jesus-Joshua returning to fulfil the prophecies of the end (cf. Mk. 13. 6), hoping to enlist Christian support. Luke seems not to have understood the point of the coincidence between Jesus and Judas, which is ruined if Theudas came first. But he may have possessed accurate information that the refusal of the Pharisees to support a policy of persecution was due to their recognition of the difference between the Church and the zealot movement, though the wording is his own and involves a serious anachronism. [Montefiore, quoted by Cadbury in *Beginnings*, 4. 278, objects that Paul's criticisms of the Pharisees show that he cannot have been educated by Gamaliel, since the rabbis taught that salvation was obtained not by keeping the Law but by repentance. But quite apart from the fact that we have no contemporary evidence of what the first-century rabbis taught, repentance only came in when there had been a failure to observe the Torah, and though rabbis no doubt admitted their own failure, there seems no reason to suppose that they regarded it as impossible to observe the Torah. (For the superiority of good works to repentance cf. Str.-B. on Mt. 4. 17 (1. 166 *ad fin.*) and Ro. 3. 20; Mishnah, P.A. 2. 1 (R. Judah the Nasi), 15 f. (R. Tarphon), 3. 13, 15 (R. Akiba), 4. 9.) The difference is that the rabbis held that repentance could make up for failures to observe the Torah, while St. Paul held that neither keeping the Torah nor repentance were of any value apart from the Cross of Christ.)[1]]

---

[1] It is possible that the correspondence between Jesus and Joshua underlies the ἀρχηγός Christology of Acts 3. 15 and 5. 31 (cf. Heb. 2. 10 and 12. 2). The word means 'originator' or 'captain' (cf. Cadbury in *Beginnings* on Acts 3. 15 and Delling in *T.W.z.N.T.*, s.voc., for its use of quasi-divine founders of colonies, and Heracl. Pont. Alleg. Hom. 34 for Heracles as ἀρχη-γὸς πάσης σοφίας). The word would thus be applicable to Joshua as the

(2) Acts 13. 38, cf. above, p. 17, n. 4. Clearly what we have here is really the substance of St. Paul's second (or later) address to any synagogue, the first having consisted of a kerygma of the O.T., leading up to the death and resurrection of Jesus as the fulfilment of the Messianic prophecies. It could only be after a second address on the abolition of the Torah implied by this that he could introduce the denunciation of v. 41; moreover, the friendly invitation to preach on the next sabbath would hardly follow a sermon which ended as this sermon ends. Luke assumes that his readers are perfectly well aware of the causes of the breach between St. Paul and the synagogue; he also assumes that they know St. Paul's teaching on the matter, if not his actual Epistles; hence he can dismiss the theme in a brief summary, which actually comes in the wrong place. The passage is fatal to any suggestion that we have an accurate verbal record of what St. Paul said on this particular occasion; it suggests, however, that we have a thoroughly reliable account of the sort of thing which he was in the habit of saying.

(3) The story of the Council of Jerusalem appears to be constructed in the same way.[1] St. Peter's language is suspiciously Pauline, but probably reflects quite accurately St. Peter's ultimate willingness to accept St. Paul's theology. On the other hand, Cadbury rightly points out that the speeches are written to suit the character of the speakers; the speech of St. James cannot be a verbal report, since its

οἰκιστής of Israel in Canaan, though it is only used in the LXX of subordinate leaders (Judges 5. 15; 1 Chron. 5. 24). Philo uses the word ἀρχηγέτης of God (De Ebr. 42), of Adam in his perfection (De Op. Mund. 142), and of Noah (De Abr. 46) as the τέλος of an old race and the ἀρχή of the new. He also uses it of purely human originators, but the word in the passages noted has a religious or mythological value which made its application to Jesus easy. The correspondence between Jesus and Joshua goes back at least as far as the book of *Testimonies* incorporated by Justin Martyr (Dial. 113. 340 c, cf. Tert. adv. Marc. 3. 16, adv. Jud. 9). It does not, however, appear in Ep. Barn. 12. 9 where we might expect it. It is at least possible that we have in the phrase a relic of a very early Christology of the Jewish Church, abandoned owing to its awkward association with false Christs. Its appearance in Hebrews would then be either a chance survival or an independent use of the term by the writer of Hebrews on account of its suitability for his Christology with its emphasis on the human example of Jesus.

[1] For the hostility between popular and Pharisaic Christianity implied in the story cf. *Jerusalem*, 225. To the evidence may be added the violently anti-Pharisaic fragment incorporated by Josephus, B.J. 1. 111. It should be remembered that the view that the ordinary Jews of Palestine really accepted the Pharisaic position rests entirely on Jos. Antt. 18. 12 ff.; but the whole treatment of the Essenes shows that his source here is ridiculously untrustworthy. In any case it only asserts that they control the Temple-service, which no doubt is true (cf. Mishnah, Yôma 1. 3 ff. (Danby 162) and Rosh-ha-Shanah 2. 9 (ib. 190)), and are generally looked up to in the towns as virtuous people.

argument depends for its validity on the fact that he quoted the LXX text of Amos. We have thus Lucan compilations to suit the speakers.

The letter of the Council is more difficult. It is written in excellent Greek (cf. Norden, *Ant. Kunstpr.* 484), but there is no reason to suppose that the Church of Jerusalem at this period could not find a perfectly competent Greek secretary. The boldness of the words 'It seemed good to the Holy Ghost and to us' is more intelligible in a genuine document of a very primitive period than in a later Lucan compilation. (For the outlook implied cf. Meyer, *Urspr. u. Anf.* 3. 185 ff. and 417.) On the other hand, the composition of letters for insertion as official documents into their narratives is a regular practice of Jewish historians (cf. Demetrius *ap.* Eus. Pr. Ev. 9. 30. 5. ff. quoting Eupolemus and Jos. Antt. 8. 51 ff. for Solomon's correspondence with Hiram; Eupolemus adds a correspondence with Pharaoh). Josephus' letters are a free paraphrase of 1 Kings 5. 3 ff., but he asserts that copies may be found in the archives of Jerusalem and Tyre; the text unfortunately differs entirely from that of Eupolemus. The Maccabean documents appear to be equally fictitious, cf. Willrich, *Judaica*, 40 ff.[1]

On the whole, the balance of probability favours the view that Luke composed the letters in accordance with general practice; but he may have copied originals.

(4) The speeches at Lystra and Athens (Acts 14. 15 and 17. 22) are excursions into the commonplaces of hellenistic philosophy from which comes the attack on temples and sacrificial cultus which Judaism was always ready to employ in order to discredit Gentile cultus, the Temple at Jerusalem being left discreetly in the background. In the speech at Athens Luke adds to his philosophical discourse a brief summary of the message of such Pauline passages as Ro. 5. Naturally the whole can be no more than a very bare summary; St. Paul on such an occasion would not have confined himself to a speech of less than a minute. I see no reason to change the view expressed in *Gentiles*, c. 1, that we have a genuine record of the occasion of St. Paul's first meeting with serious Gentile philosophy, and that the speech embodies the kind of philosophical commonplaces that he was likely to know and use. (To the parallels from popular philosophy quoted there add Ps.-Heracl. Ep. 4; Philo, Q.D.P.I.S. 20 (from a pagan source); Zeno *ap.* Diog. Laert. 7. 33, more fully in Clem. Alex. Strom. 5. 11. 76 (691 P.) and Plut. De Tranq. Anim. 20 (477 *c*).) In general de Zwaan in *H.T.R.* 17. 2 (1924), 132 ff., seems correct in his view of the speech; his doubts as to the Christology seem unfounded, since it is simply that of Ro. 1. 3. His objection to τὸ θεῖον is also unfounded in view of the frequency of the phrase in Philo (cf. Leisegang's index) and Josephus (*passim*, e. g. Antt. 18. 5, 20. 41). St. Paul does not use it in his letters to converts, but this does not

[1] Bickermann, *Der Gott der Makkabäer*, 175, attempts to discredit Willrich's view; I cannot feel that his attempt is successful in view of the Jewish predilection for forged documents in the hellenistic era.

prove that he would not have thought it suitable for an audience of philosophers. It is of course perfectly possible that it comes from Luke rather than from St. Paul himself.

(5) It has been objected that 20. 35 proves that Acts in its present form cannot be the work of Luke, Paul's companion, but must come from an editor of his reminiscences, since St. Paul is made to quote a logion which is not in the Gospel (cf. Windisch in *Beginnings*, 2. 331). This betrays a complete failure to understand his methods. If Luke only picked up this floating saying after his Gospel had been completed and thought this a suitable place to insert it, he would not have hesitated to do so in the supposed interests of 'consistency'. It remains possible that St. Paul used it on this occasion or some other, but the position of the logion outside the Gospel suggests that Luke only heard of it after the Gospel was written. The authenticity of the saying depends on the source; we cannot say what its value was.

(6) 26. 24 is a clear case of Lucan composition. Festus suggests, whether seriously or not, that St. Paul's studies have driven him mad, implying that he has been quoting from a number of 'writings'. The interruption would be appropriate after a long string of testimonies from the prophets or supposed testimonies to Jewish monotheism from pagan writers. But we have not had such a string of quotations, though it is possible that we are intended to read them into v. 22. But the real point is that just as the Pauline Gospel is a 'stumbling-block to the Jews', who therefore interrupt appropriately at the mission to the Gentiles in 22. 22, so it is foolishness to the Greeks; hence Festus is represented appropriately as interrupting at the same point. But Festus could hardly object to the idea of preaching to the Gentiles, and so this point is coupled with the doctrine that Christ must suffer and rise from the dead. Festus' interruption may well be genuine; it is the sort of thing which St. Paul (or Luke if he was present) could easily remember. But Luke has omitted the testimonies which alone would explain Festus' interruption.

In this speech the introduction of 'in the Hebrew tongue' as an apology for the barbarous name 'Saul' is more likely to come from Luke, though it is conceivable that St. Paul would apologize in this way. Cadbury (*Beginnings*, ad loc.) objects that 'it is hard for thee to kick against the pricks' is a purely Greek proverb; but Ps. Sol. 16. 4 suggests that it may have been acclimatized in Judaism, and such a proverb might well have found its way into a collection of proverbs available for Jewish students of Greek.

In general, the speeches suggest that we have occasional reminiscences of genuine Pauline utterances, worked into free compositions of the sort of thing which Luke regarded as appropriate for the occasion. These compositions may of course include reminiscences of speeches heard on other occasions, but it is probable that the greater part is Luke's own composition, which is on the whole remarkably successful.

LECTURE II

HITHERTO we have been considering passages in which, for the most part, the Greek style suggested an alien element imposed on the original Palestinian tradition of the Gospel and the early stories of its dissemination. But long before our Gospels and the Acts had reached their present form a Christian literature had begun to make its appearance which was the product of the mixed Jewish-hellenistic culture which was to be found in all the larger cities of the eastern Mediterranean world. That culture was not only confined to the Judaism of the Dispersion. In a curiously neglected passage of the Talmud[1] R. Gamaliel is reported as saying that his father R. Simeon b. Gamaliel II had in his house 500 lads learning the wisdom of the Jews and another 500 learning the wisdom of the Greeks. The number of the pupils at this academy are of course as ludicrous as all ancient Jewish statistics; but there is no reason to doubt that the rabbis of the first century A.D. were alive to the need of such a dual curriculum. It was customary to invite visitors to address the synagogues of the Dispersion; it may already have been customary for emissaries to be sent from Palestine to visit those synagogues and to encourage them to persevere in their faith.[2] The prestige of Jerusalem would demand that such emissaries should be able to speak in a style which educated Jews and interested Gentiles would regard as reasonably good, and Jewish interests would demand speakers who could represent them attractively before Gentile magistrates. Jewish preachers would further need a smattering of popular philosophy, particularly of that mixture of Stoicism and Platonism which was peculiarly congenial to Jewish missionary propaganda, and a knowledge of Greek literature so far as it could be derived from popular handbooks; it would seem that Judaism had its own

[1] Sotah 49 b.

[2] It is clear from Acts 13. 15, 17. 2, 18. 4 that distinguished visitors were likely to be invited to address the synagogue. I cannot find evidence for systematic sending of emissaries from Palestine earlier than Justin Martyr, Dial. 17 (234 e), 108 (335 c). But there was close contact between Jerusalem and the Jews living in the great Gentile cities, cf. Jos. Antt. 17. 300 (B.J. 2. 80), Vita 13 f. Tertullus, the ῥήτωρ of Acts 24. 1, appears to be a Jew trained as a professional advocate in Greek courts. Presumably Josephus' visit to Rome in A.D. 64 (Vita 13, cf. Schürer, G.J.V. 1. 75) was due to similar reasons: his knowledge of Greek would qualify him as an advocate. Naturally he represents his journey as due to his personal piety, but this need not be taken seriously. Cf. also Schlatter, Gesch. Israels³, 16 f.

compilations of this type, composed of real or alleged extracts from the great writers of antiquity, designed to prove that the wisdom of the Greeks really taught an ethical monotheism, derived by unacknowledged borrowing from Moses. The poets were made to support the philosophers in the interests of Judaism; it was of course no objection that many of the extracts were the production of Jewish imitators.[1]

Thus the circumstances would demand that the rabbis should encourage some of their more promising pupils in the study of Greek culture of this type; there is no difficulty in supposing that Paul acquired all his knowledge of Greek in this way during his education 'at the feet of Gamaliel'.[2] It was in this Graeco-Jewish atmosphere, which it seems could exist in Jerusalem itself, that the Gospel was translated into the terms of hellenistic theology. As an introduction to that atmosphere it is worth studying a passage in which St. Paul gives us an excellent sample both of the conventional philosophy borrowed by the Jews from the Greeks and also his ability to write in what was regarded as a fine style in some circles.

The passage is Ro. 1. 18 ff. After an apologetic opening Paul breaks off abruptly to proclaim the wrath of God against mankind for their failure to recognize Him from His works. The pompous denunciation ἀποκαλύπτεται γὰρ ὀργὴ θεοῦ may have been borrowed from epistolary convention.[3] The arguments are throughout those which the synagogue had learnt from popular Greek philosophy and turned into commonplaces, that the existence of God can be inferred from His works,[4] that He

---

[1] Cf. Schürer, *G.J.V.* 3. 595.

[2] He himself always insists that he was educated at Jerusalem, and his whole knowledge of Greek thought, literature, and language is that of Judaism. He could no doubt have got a similar Jewish-Greek education in many other cities of the ancient world, including Tarsus. There is not a scrap of evidence that he had any knowledge of Greek apart from the common stock of hellenistic Judaism, and there is no reason to suppose that he could not have acquired this at Jerusalem and that his claim to have been educated there is untrue.

[3] At any rate, it is strikingly reminiscent of Pap. Par. 2388, col. ix, 47 (= Wilcken, *U.P.Z.* i. 626) ἀπόκειται γὰρ παρὰ θεῶν μῆνις τοῖς μὴ κατὰ τὸ βέλτιστον προαιρουμένοις ζῆν. Wilcken holds the letter to be a copy of an actual letter by a pupil to whom it had been given as a pattern of literary style in letter-writing. He remarks on the words quoted: 'This pompous sentence reminds me again of the memorial of Nemrud-Dagh' οἷς ἀποκείσεται παρὰ θεῶν καὶ ἡρώων χάρις εὐσεβείας.

[4] Xenophon, Mem. 1. 4. 3 ff.; Corp. Herm. 5. 6 ff.; Ps.-Arist. De Mundo 6. 25; and in Judaism Wisd. 13. 5; Philo, De Decal. 59 f. and *passim*.

cannot be represented by any anthropomorphic image, still less
by the likeness of anything lower in the corruptible order,[1] and
that the corruption of worship into idolatry was the inevitable
cause of the moral corruption of the Gentile world.[2] It is not
only the matter that is drawn from the stock homiletic of the
synagogue, familiar to the readers; the form is a deliberate
parody of the portentous grandiloquence with which the synagogue preacher encouraged his Jewish hearers to thank God
that they were not as other men are and to encourage the
Gentiles among them to become proselytes. The conventional
list of vices is decorated with some typical assonances thrown in
to relieve its monotony, and works up to an excellent piece of
well-balanced rhythmical writing in v. 30 f., closing with
a double cretic with the last long syllable of the first resolved.[3]
The whole of this portentous inflation is brought down in ruins
by the three rapier-like sentences with which c. 2 opens; it is the
Jew not the Gentile who deserves the heaviest condemnation,
since he is as great a sinner as the Gentile but with less excuse;
even here it would seem that St. Paul has modelled his plain
speaking on the rhetorical tradition of the preachers of Cynic
philosophy.[4] From this he reverts to his more elaborate style,

[1] For a collection of Greek condemnations of images going back as far as
Xenophanes cf. Bevan, *Holy Images*, 64 ff.; for the text of Xenophanes cf.
Diels, *Fr. d. Vors.*[1] 53. 11 ff. and 55. 23. The corruptibility of man and all
created things as part of the argument against making images of God who
is incorruptible reappears in Philo, Leg. ad Gaium 118, though curiously
enough not in the skilfully balanced contrast between the impotence of idols
and the powers with which men credit them in Wisd. 13. 17 ff.

[2] This seems to be an adaptation of the argument of Theophrastus (*ap.*
Porph. *ap.* Eus. Pr. Ev. 4. 14. 1 f.) with a more elaborated version of the
same moral, namely that errors in religion lead to general degradation both
in religion and conduct. Cf. Philo, De Decal. 80, where we are told that the
visitor to Egypt pities the Egyptians whose worship of beasts has turned them
into beasts in human shape, and De Virt. (De Paen.) 181, where the
penitent (i.e. the proselyte to Judaism) immediately develops all the virtues
while the Jew who falls away develops all the vices.

For the whole dependence of Jewish and Christian apologetic on the
commonplaces of Greek popular philosophy cf. Geffcken, *Zwei griechische
Apologeten*, intr., pp. xvii ff. The absurdity of the Egyptian worship of idols
was of course a commonplace, and St. Paul might have drawn it from any
manual of Jewish apologetic, not necessarily from the book of Wisdom.

[3] Cf. above, p. 5, n. 2. The assonances φόνου φθόνου . . . ἀσυνέτους ἀσυνθέ-
τους are typical: the rhythmical effect is very successful: ἀνελεήμονας ψιθυριστὰς
καταλάλους | θεοστυγεῖς ὑβριστὰς | ὑπερηφάνους ἀλαζόνας | ἐφευρετὰς κακῶν | γονεῦσιν
ἀπειθεῖς | ἀσυνέτους ἀσυνθέτους | ἀστόργους ἀνελεημόνας (— ‿ ‿ ‿ | ‿ —).

[4] Note the assonance κρίνεις, κρίνων, κατακρίνεις, κρίνων in 2. 1 and the address

and to the commonplaces of Jewish-hellenistic philosophy, which had found in the Stoic idea of the wise man as the ἔμψυχος νόμος a convenient method of explaining how it was that the patriarchs were righteous although ignorant of the Torah, and was also familiar with the idea of conscience as a witness for the defence or the prosecution.[1] The good and rather ambitious style is well maintained until the end of v. 20, at which St. Paul reaches the end of a very complicated protasis to his conditional sentence and breaks down woefully with the abrupt series of questions which replace the apodosis. Even these are structurally well balanced; but by now we have reached the real point of the letter, the Pauline doctrine of the relation of the Law to the Gospel, and he is far too seriously concerned with his subject to have any regard for style.[2]

Now all this is the kind of thing which any intelligent young Jew would receive as the proper method for preaching to educated Jews of the Dispersion or the Gentile hearers who were to be found in almost every synagogue; we have direct evidence in the Talmud that such instruction was given at Jerusalem by R. Gamaliel II: it would have been no less needed in the days of R. Gamaliel I, and there is no need to weave elaborate theories as to St. Paul's education in the Greek schools of Tarsus[3] or as to the possibility of his having become acquainted in that city with the mysteries of Mithras.[4] He has a superficial knowledge of popular philosophy; he can write good rhetorical Greek

of an imaginary opponent after the fashion of the diatribe for which cf. the references in Schenkl's index to the text of Epictetus to the word ἄνθρωπε.

[1] For vv. 4 ff. as a specimen of Asiatic rhetoric cf. Norden, op. cit. 507, and note the assonance in 11 ff. For the good man as the unwritten law cf. Diotogenes ap. Stob. Anth. 2. 260 (48. 61) (apparently 1st cent. B.C.; cf. Bréhier, Les Idées philosophiques ... de Philon, 19), Dion. Halic. Antt. Rom. 7. 41, Philo, De Vit. Moys. 2. 4 (following Diotogenes or a similar source), De Abr. 5. For the ideas of v. 14 f. cf. Philo, De Post. Cain 59, De Spec. Leg. 1. 235, and cf. p. 82.

[2] None the less as against Lightfoot's argument (Galatians, 45 ff.) that the similarity of Gal. and Ro. proves that they were written at about the same time, it is instructive to notice that the style of Ro. is consistently better than that of Gal. Thus the antithesis μέν ... δέ occurs twice in Gal. and 14 times in Ro.; the relative length of the Epistles would naturally give us a proportion of 2 to 7, not 2 to 14. This is symptomatic of the general difference between the tempestuous polemic of Gal. and the ordered exposition of Ro. Gal. is written in the heat of a living controversy which has been decided when Ro. is written.

[3] As Ramsay does in Hastings, D.B. 4. 685.

[4] Cf. Clemen, Religionsgesch. Erkl. d. N.T.² 35 f.

of the Asiatic type when he remembers to do so, but he is quite
incapable of sustaining it when he is carried away by his enthusiasm. He has a smattering of Greek literature drawn from
anthologies for the guidance of the preacher or controversialist,[1]
and his citizenship of Tarsus is merely a matter of social distinction to be used if occasion should demand it.[2]

From the point of view of the theology of the New Testament
it is the philosophy of hellenistic Judaism that is of most interest.
Its main exponent is of course Philo, and at first sight there
could seem to be nothing so remote from the frigid pedantries
of Philo as the flaming enthusiasm of the N.T. writers. As a
philosopher Philo is negligible; as a writer he achieved a dull-
ness which is portentous. He begins to be interesting when we
realize that he has incorporated a whole mass of material, which
would otherwise have been lost, from which we can reconstruct
the attempt of Judaism to convert the Gentile world. The
Church inevitably took over this method of commending the
Gospel, and from this point of view Philo is of enormous importance for the study of St. Paul and the later N.T. writers,
especially of the Fourth Gospel.

That Philo is not an original thinker but a compiler is clear
not only from his total lack of original thought but from the
slovenliness with which he incorporates his material. He has in
at least two places retained language which implies the truth of

---

[1] For Acts 17. 28 and 1 Cor. 15. 23 cf. *Gentiles*, 90, n. 5. Whether the
former quotation be due to Paul or not, it is drawn from an anthology of this
type. The author of Titus 1. 12 drew on a similar source for his quotation
from Epimenides (imitated by Callimachus, Hymn. ad Jov. 8. 9), the Cretan
habit of lying being referred to their claim to show the tomb of Zeus who
is immortal. (For the relation of Epimenides and Callimachus cf. Diels, *Fr.
d. Vors.* 502 f.) The tomb of Zeus in Crete was a stock argument of the
Academics against traditional religion (Cic. de Nat. Deor. 3. 21. 53), and
so passed into the armoury of Jewish and Christian apologists (Tat. ad
Graecos 27; Minucius Felix, Oct. 21. 8; Firm. Mat. De Err. prof. Rel. 7. 6;
Athenagoras, Leg. pro Christ. 30. 158 (with a polemic against Callimachus
for denying that there is a tomb of Zeus); Clem. Alex. Protr. 2. 37 (32 P.)
(where Callimachus' reference to the tomb is mentioned but his denial
ignored); Or. Sib. 8. 48, quoted by Lact. Div. Inst. 1. 11. 45; Tert. Apol. 25;
Eus. Pr. Ev. 3. 10. 14). It appears from Lact., loc. cit., that the tomb of Zeus
figured in Ennius' translation of Euhemerus. The quotation in Titus really
belongs to an orthodox Gentile use of Callimachus against Gentile sceptics
or Jewish-Christian apologetics: it has thus found its way into Christian
circles.

[2] For a similar claim to social distinction rather than legal status by a
defendant cf. P. Cair. 10440 (Mitteis u. Wilcken, *Chrestom. d. pap. Urk.* 1. 2. 27
ἐγὼ μὲν οὔκ εἰμι Δοῦλος . . . ἀλλὰ Διασήμου πόλεως Ἀλεξανδρείας γυμνασίαρχος).

the pagan mythology of his Gentile sources; elsewhere his treatment of the use of the name of God reveals that he is using Jewish material dating from quite different stages in the gradual development by which Judaism suppressed the pronunciation of the name in public worship and all the reputable parts of life.[1] Again his use of the O.T. outside the Pentateuch is inexplicable except on the view that he is incorporating material of different dates, most of which goes back to a period when only the Pentateuch had been translated into Greek. He is simply a compiler of the traditional midrashic material of the schools and synagogues of Alexandria.[2] It is this that gives him his importance for the study of the N.T. For however remote the atmosphere of Philo may be from the rustic synagogues of Galilee, it need not have been very remote from the rabbinical academies of Jerusalem or the schools of the Dispersion in the west. The surprising similarities between Philo and the N.T. are thus intelligible, since both go back to a common tradition of hellenistic Jewish interpretation of the O.T. to the Greek world. The differences represent the difference between the religion of the primitive Church and a peculiarly pedantic exposition of the Judaism of Alexandria.

From this point of view we may look at the method of using an O.T. text which is common to St. Paul and Philo. We cannot read Romans without feeling that St. Paul reads a good deal into his favourite proof-text 'Abraham believed God and it was counted to him for righteousness'. But it is nothing to what Philo reads into it; for it is also a favourite proof-text of his and he uses it some eight times. It is one of the texts which owed its popularity to its obvious difficulty; the antisemitic scoffer naturally objected that any sensible person would believe God, so why should Abraham be counted righteous for doing so?[3] It is a favourite device of the Alexandrine school to use an obvious difficulty as an excuse for reading into the passage a hidden spiritual meaning of peculiar importance.[4] So, says Philo, it is

---

[1] In the form Iao the name is so frequent in the magical papyri that it must have continued in magic long after it had been abandoned in worship; but it is possible that 'Iao' was at least in some instances taken over from genuine Jewish religion before the pronunciation of the name was abandoned. (For the date of these texts and their relation to religion cf. Nock in *Journal of Egyptian Archaeology*, xv. 219 ff.) Cf. *Judaism*, i. 424 f.

[2] For Philo's methods of compilation cf. Note to this lecture.

[3] Q.R.D.H. 90.

[4] For the method cf. *Gentiles*, 83 and 104, n. 2. To the examples noted may be added De Somn. i. 93, De Ebr. 65, De Spec. Leg. i. 327.

no small thing to refuse to trust in external things and to believe in God alone. So it is possible to represent Abraham as the true philosopher who passes from idolatry to astrology and from astrology to the finding of the one true God, succeeding where Socrates failed.[1] His faith, the first recorded in history,[2] was the reward of his faithful quest, and was naturally accounted to him for the righteousness which it really was. Elsewhere the verse is made a text for a panegyric on faith as the sure means of escaping from the troubles of the world, which closely resembles a certain type of popular Christian literature;[3] we have nothing resembling the Pauline view of faith, though once we come near to that of Heb. 11.[4] Thus the apparent absurdity of the text is made to prove that rightly understood it contains a promise of reward to the seeker, i.e. the potential proselyte. It is a favourite missionary text, and St. Paul adapts it for his own purposes; he has the advantage of not having to explain it away as Philo has to do. Abraham's faith was simply a submission to God, similar to St. Paul's own submission on the road to Damascus and that which every convert had to make; St. Paul's view of justification by faith enables him to accept the text instead of explaining it away. Similarly the short midrash on the patriarchs in Ro. 9. 1 ff. is entirely Philonic; Philo uses the theme to glorify Israel for their descent from such men, God's preference for the highly unattractive Jacob being due to his foreknowledge that Jacob would be righteous and Esau wicked.[5] The implied difficulty is evaded by the assumption that God's foreknowledge does not imply predestination; once again St. Paul has in his favour the fact that he is interpreting the scriptures in their literal sense, not explaining them away;[6] the difficulties of his own theology do not here concern us.

[1] Leg. Alleg. 3. 228. Q.D.S.I. 4, De Abr. 276; cf. my article in *H.T.R.* 28. 1. 55.

[2] Cf. R. Simeon b. Abba (*c.* A.D. 280) in Exod. R. 23. 85*a* (Str.-B. 3. 200), an interesting point of contact between Philo and the rabbis.

[3] De Abr. 268.

[4] De Migr. Abr. 44, where faith believes ἤδη παρεῖναι τὰ μὴ παρόντα. The verbal parallel to Ro. 4. 17 is interesting since in both we are dealing with the same theme, Abraham's faith that God will give him a son.

[5] De Virt. 206 ff.; De Praem. et Poen. 58 ff.

[6] Note also the considerable verbal similarity between Rom. 9. 19 and Wisd. 12. 12 where God gives the Canaanites time to repent, although He knows they will not do so. Another instance of St. Paul's use of favourite Philonic texts is Ro. 10. 6 ff., for which cf. *Gentiles*, 102; for 1 Cor. 10. 1 ff. cf. *Gentiles*, 122; for Gen. 2. 7 in 1 Cor. 15. 45 cf. ib. 81 and 127; for Lev. 26. 11 ff. in 2 Cor. 6. 16 cf. *Jerusalem*, 290, n. 4; for Deut. 21. 23 in Gal. 3. 13 cf. *Gentiles*, 108.

Thus the close connexion between the Greek schools of Jerusalem and those of Alexandria appears in their use of a common stock of proof-texts. It can equally be found in their use of popular philosophy. Both St. Paul and Philo have an essentially superficial acquaintance with Greek thought; they are completely indifferent to philosophy as such, and only employ it as a handmaid in the service of a revealed religion which they have accepted for reasons which have nothing to do with philosophy. Philo's knowledge is of course infinitely wider in range than St. Paul's so far as we can judge; it is also far less Jewish: but it is equally superficial. It must be remembered that most of the 'philosophy' of the time was a 'theology' in the sense that it was concerned not with the discovery of truth but with the vindication of religion; philosophy is a means of explaining away the crudities of popular religion and substituting for them a theology which can claim the allegiance of the wise and learned.[1]

It is this adaptation of Christianity to the general theistic scheme of the first century, particularly by the author of the Fourth Gospel, that will concern us during the rest of these lectures; but it was from the current practice of the synagogues that the Church took over the tradition, which Judaism had taken over from the popular philosophy that was the common property of all intelligent people who were not Epicureans or Sceptics. We will begin with the conception of Jesus, the Messiah of the primitive Church as the divine Logos, the agent of God in the creation and preservation of the cosmos.

It is well known that the general desire of the hellenistic age was to find gods who were 'saviours'. 'Salvation' might take many forms. At its lowest it is represented by the ode of Hermocles addressed to Demetrius Poliorcetes at Athens, perhaps the nadir of human religion.[2] At a somewhat higher stage it produces the cult of a particular ruler as the 'saviour' of society; even Philo can describe Augustus as Soter and Euergetes, though normally such titles are reserved for the God of Israel and only applied sarcastically to rulers.[3] But at its best the cult of a

[1] Cf. Plut. De Is. et Os. 8 (353 e); Cornutus, Epidr. 35 ad fin.

[2] Athenaeus, Deipn. 6. 253 d and 697 a; Anth. Lyr. 2. 249 ff. Some of it might almost be a parody of Jewish or Christian piety (b. 15 ff.): 'For all the other gods are far off, or they have no ears to hear, or they are not, or they care not for us one whit. But we see thee whole, not made of wood or stone, but in very truth (ἀληθινόν).'

[3] For a saviour king in the Ptolemaic age, cf. Publ. de la soc. R. égypt. 1. Ἐντεύξεις, 11. 6, where a Ptolemy of the third century B.C. is described as τὸν

saviour could rise above man's immediate needs of peace, health, and prosperity; a particular deity could be regarded as the manifestation of God in the cosmos, and be addressed by the votary in more or less monotheistic language as the saviour both of the worshipper and of the whole universe or one particular aspect of it. As a saviour in this sense he could be equated with the Logos or one of the Logoi through which the supreme deity ordered the universe, or with the supreme deity himself; which position was given him depended on his traditional position in the Pantheon or on the extent to which the worshipper was concerned to observe the proprieties of Stoic-Platonic theology.[1]

πάντων κοινὸν σωτῆρα. For Julius Caesar as κοινὸν τοῦ ἀνθρωπίνου βίου σωτῆρα and Nero as σωτὴρ καὶ εὐεργέτης τῆς οἰκουμένης cf. *Voc. Gr. N.T.*, s.voc. σωτήρ. Philo, In Flacc. 74, definitely describes Augustus as ὁ σωτήρ καὶ εὐεργέτης in a passage recording his recognition of the Jewish Gerousia at Alexandria. Cf. ib. 126 for the application of such titles to Flaccus himself by his Egyptian subjects who have since his fall become his accusers. There is a similar sarcastic usage in Leg. ad Gaium 22, but this is from a pagan source, cf. Note. It would seem that occasionally the Jews of Alexandria could allow political exigencies to override theological propriety; normally such titles are reserved for God alone, e.g. De Sobr. 55, where God is Δεσπότης καὶ εὐεργέτης of the αἰσθητὸς κόσμος, and σωτήρ καὶ εὐεργέτης (not Δεσπότης or κύριος) of the νοητὸς κόσμος.

[1] For the variations in the Stoic systems cf. Diog. Laert. 7. 135 (where God is purely an immanent principle) and 147, where he is both a transcendent creator and an immanent logos. For the inconsistency of Chrysippus and Antipater of Tarsus in this point cf. Plut. De Stoic. Rep. 38, 1951*f.* Ps.-Arist. De Mundo 6. 6 f. abandons the divine immanence as bringing God into unseemly places, but in 6. 16 we find a divine 'power' imparted by God to the aether and passing through it to the remoter parts of the cosmos. For this work cf. Lietzmann, *Gesch. d. alt. Kirche*, 1. 180 ff.; here we have a transcendentalized form of the Stoic view (Cic. De Nat. Deor. 2. 11. 29 ff.) that the cosmos is a divine, living, and intelligent whole supplying life and intelligence to its parts. Philo's sources are drawn from the transcendental type; a pure immanentism could find no place in Judaism.

For a saviour as a logos cf. Aristides, Or. 42 (6). 4 (Keil, 2. 335), where Asclepius is described as τὸ πᾶν ἄγων καὶ νέμων, σωτὴρ τῶν ὅλων ... σώζων τά τε ὄντα ἀεὶ καὶ τὰ γιγνόμενα: he is both Asclepius and yet is Ζεὺς 'Ασκλήπιος and one with Zeus. The resemblance to Philo's Logos is obvious: for Aristides' language cf. such passages as Philo, De Cher. 36 (cf. the Son as Logos in Heb. 1. 3), except that Philo does not appear to describe the Logos as σωτήρ, perhaps because the title might suggest that he was to be regarded too definitely as a subordinate deity. (But in Wisd. 9. 18 ff. we have practically an aretalogy of Wisdom as the Saviour of Israel in history, though the actual title is not employed.) Cf. also the dream of Aristides in Ἱεροὶ Λόγοι 4. 56 (Keil, 2. 439). It would be impossible to distinguish the world-soul of Aristides' Platonist friend here from the Logos in such passages as De Fug. et Inv. 110, De Plant. 9, and though in De Migr. Abr. 179 Philo rejects the

Heracles is a particularly interesting specimen of this theology. Since Isocrates had held him up as a model for the kings of Macedonia[1] he had been a saviour who had rid the world of barbarism and established civilization.[2] But he could also be the Logos which gives strength and cohesion to the cosmos,[3] or in virtue of his death on Mount Oeta he could be the pure principle of fire through which God proceeded out of Himself into the creation of the cosmos, to return at the end of each world period into Himself.[4] If the contrast between the mythical figure and the divine Logos was felt to be too strong, it was possible to prove from ancient mythology the existence of a divine Heracles as distinct from the human;[5] the latter was the son of Alcmena, who had earned the right to the divine name by his noble deeds.[6] But the difficulty was not really serious, for allegory could explain anything to the pious votary who only desired to continue to practise religion without feeling too severely its inconsistency with a more or less monotheistic system of philosophy.[7]

This conception of Heracles goes back at least as far as Seneca.[8]

idea of a world-soul as implying a deification of the cosmos and associated with astrology, yet in De Somn. 1. 2 one class of dreams is produced by the correspondence between man's soul and the world-soul (? from Posidonius, cf. Cic. De Div. 1. 49. 110; Chalcidius, ad Tim. 251; St. vet. Frr. 2. 344), while in Leg. Alleg. 1. 91 God is the soul of the universe. Here Asclepius, who could never be the supreme deity, is described in language which gives him the place of the Logos in Philo; in Aristides' panegyric on Sarapis Or. 45 (8) (Keil, 2. 358) we find similar connexions with Philo's language about the Logos. Thus he combines the 'powers' of all the gods, cf. De Somn. 1. 2. Sarapis in this speech appears as a 'saviour' (33). For providence as the Logos of God governing the 'powers' of fate and necessity cf. Corp. Herm. Exc. 12 (Stob. 1. 5. 20; Scott, 1. 434).

[1] Phil. 109 (Blass, 1. 119), cf. Kärst, Gesch. d. Hellenismus, 144.

[2] Diod. Sic. 4. 8. 5; Epict. Diss. 2. 16. 44, 3. 26. 32; Philo, Leg. ad G. 81, 90; Seneca, De Benef. 1. 13. 3.

[3] Cornutus, Epidr. 31 (St. vet. Frr. 1. 115, where v. Arnim's emendation of λόγος to τόνος is quite unnecessary).

[4] Seneca, De Benef. 4. 8. 1, where Liber is Jupiter as the source of life, Hercules Jupiter as sustaining all things and returning into fire, and Mercury Jupiter as the source of reason.

[5] Cf. the Cretan mythology of Diod. Sic. 5. 76. 1.

[6] Cornutus, loc. cit., apparently going back to Cleanthes and with a polemical note against those who confound the human 'saviour' with the Logos.

[7] For religion of this type cf. v. Arnim, Dio v. Prusa, 479. For the difficulty and the way out cf. Diod. Sic. 4. 8. 5, where πατροπαράδοτος εὐσέβεια is curiously similar to 1 Pet. 1. 18 (a Jewish-Christian criticism of a common defence of paganism?).

[8] Cf. above, n. 4. A similar thought may underlie De Clem. 2. 2. 1, where

Now Heracles was the patron of the Stoic and Cynic philosophers[1] and it was with this type of philosophy that Judaism
had the closest affinity.[2] It is possible that Judaism had learnt
from its allegorical interpretation of Heracles the σωτήρ as a
cosmic λόγος, the possibility of substituting the divine Logos for
the awkward figure of the Jewish Messiah, who was quite out
of place in a Judaism which tried to be a system of philosophy.
Philo has consistently eliminated eschatology and the Messiah
from his writings,[3] and in view of his carelessness in revising his
sources, this can only mean that the whole tradition of Alexandrine teaching had done so for him. But in one passage[4] he
interprets Zech. 6 12 'behold a man whose name is the sunrising' as the text runs in the LXX (Heb. 'branch') with a
distinctly controversial note; 'it would be a strange thing to call
a man the sunrising, but it is not strange if it refers to the
immaterial man, who is identical with the image of God, the
eldest son raised up by the Father of all, elsewhere named
the first-born.' This is just a conventional string of names for
the Logos; but there is no reason why it should be strange to
describe the Messiah as the sun or the sunrise; there is ample

Nero is the head which supplies strength and health to the empire which
is his body (for the passage cf. *Gentiles*, 162), much as Heracles supplies
strength to the cosmos in Cornutus. Now in Dio Chrys. 1. 84 (v. Arn.
1. 16) Heracles owes his title of saviour to the fact that he was and is a destroyer of tyrants and an upholder of kings καὶ βοηθός ἐστι καὶ φύλαξ σοι τῆς
ἀρχῆς ἕως ἂν τυγχάνῃς βασιλεύων (the speech is addressed to Trajan according
to v. Arnim, *Dio v. Prusa*, 325). For Heracles as a deliverer from tyrants
cf. Epict. Diss. 3. 26. 32. It would be easy to change this conception into
that of Heracles as the Logos of right government, and it is possible that
Seneca has simply substituted Nero for Heracles.

  [1] Lucian, Conv. 16; the tradition goes back to Antisthenes (Diog. Laert.
6. 2) and Prodicus' story of the choice of Heracles, Xen. Mem. 2. 1. 21.

  [2] The most notable instance is Philo's Quod Omnis Probus Liber, a Stoic-
Cynic diatribe adapted to Judaism. Note the glorification of Zeno (who of
course was copying Moses) in 53 and 57, Antisthenes (28), Calanus (96),
Anaxarchus and Zeno of Elea (105); the last three all reappear in Cicero,
Tusc. Disp. 2. 22. 52; in Philo's original the theme is expanded by a glorification of Heracles based on Eur. Fr. 687 f. Cf. also his panegyric of Diogenes
(121 and also in Q.D.S.I. 146 and De Gig. 33; there are also unacknowledged borrowings in Q.O.P.L. 40 and 42). The popularity of the theme
in Philonic circles is shown by the use of Zeno of Elea and Anaxarchus as
an argument against providence by the objector in De Prov. 2. 10 (A 51).
Cf. Wendland, *Philo u. d. kynisch-stoische Diatribe*, 62 f. and *passim*, and
Bréhier, *Id. Phil. . . . de Philon*, 252 and 261.

  [3] Cf. *Gentiles*, 27.

  [4] De Conf. Ling. 62.

precedent for this, going back to Mal. 4. 2.[1] It would seem that in this case at least Judaism had followed Gentile theology in equating its 'saviour' with the divine Logos and so eliminating the awkward figure of the Messiah, just as St. Paul does when he represents Jesus not simply as the Messiah who is shortly to wind up the world-process, but as the divine Wisdom who was the agent of creation. St. Paul is not indebted to the Alexandrines, since he does not use the term Logos, which would have been far more convenient than the feminine Wisdom which he uses in 1 Cor. 1. 24. It is at least possible that the Greek schools of Jerusalem were already accustomed to the substitution of the creative Wisdom of Prov. 8 for the Messiah in preaching to the Greek world, Wisdom again being equated with the Torah,[2] though it remains possible that St. Paul arrived independently at the equation of the Messiah with the Logos on the strength of ideas which were generally current at the time when he wrote. It is probable that this equation was decisive for the preservation of monotheism. Jesus as the creative Logos-Wisdom of Judaism could be represented as one with the supreme God; as a saviour he would in the hellenistic world have been in danger of becoming merely one of many saviours.

It was perhaps a feeling of this danger that is responsible for the rarity with which Jesus is described as a 'saviour' until we come to the very latest books of the N.T., although Christianity is essentially a religion of salvation. We do indeed find it in Luke's infancy narrative, where we have a thoroughly Jewish document, representing the Jewish version of that expectation of salvation which was common to the Mediterranean world at

[1] For the Messiah as the sun cf. Dölger, *Sol Salutis*, 155, and for Zech. 6. 12 as a Messianic text cf. Justin Martyr, Dial. c. Tryph. 106 (334 *b*) and 121 (350 *a*), drawn from the collection of testimonia which Justin inserts in his supposed dialogue; it may be noted that he follows the LXX 'Sunrise' not the Hebrew 'branch'. For the rabbinical interpretations of the text as Messianic cf. Talm. Jer. Ber. 2. 4 *ad fin.* (Tr. Schwab. 44), Lam. R. on 1. 16 (Buber's ed. p. 88 *ad fin.*), Yalk. Sim. 64 (p. 35 *b* of the Warsaw ed. of 1875).

[2] For Wisdom=Torah cf. *Gentiles*, 60 and 69. Hoskyns and Davey, *The Fourth Gospel*, 155, ask 'How is it that the wealth of imagery descriptive of the glory of Wisdom has been transferred to honour the Word?' The simple reason is that neither has any real function in Judaism, and the Logos is simply a later name for the earlier Wisdom, cf. *Gentiles*, 57 ff. and 114, n. 4. It must be remembered that the sole *raison d'être* both of Wisdom and the Logos was to make Judaism intellectually respectable in Gentile circles; neither figure plays any real part in Philo or in any other Jewish writer. Cf. Philo, De Mund. Op. 170 ff., where the advantages of the Stoic-Platonic cosmogony contain no reference to the Logos.

the time.[1] We find it also in Acts 5. 31, which seems to contain a very primitive Jewish-Christian Christology, and in Acts 13. 23, where He is specifically the Jewish Messiah of the house of David in St. Paul's address to the Jews of Antioch in Pisidia. St. Paul only uses the word once;[2] it does not appear in the Mark and Q tradition; it occurs in Eph. 5. 23, a fairly late book where Jesus as the saviour of the body distinctly suggests such deities as Sarapis and Asclepius.[3] Otherwise the term is mainly used in the Pastoral Epistles dating from a time when the Church was sufficiently sure of its position to use the language of Gentile religion without endangering the faith of its members. It is at least possible that 'the grace of God which bringeth salvation' and teaches us to look for the glorious epiphany of our Lord and Saviour Jesus Christ (Tit. 2. 11 ff., cf. 2 Tim. 1. 8 ff.) is a deliberate application of the conventional language of the imperial cultus applied to Jesus as a contradiction of all that cultus implied.[4] Apart from these documents it appears only once in John 4. 42, a passage which is significant as a specimen of the methods of the evangelist, and forms an appropriate introduction to the study of the Fourth Gospel.[5] The title 'saviour of the world' is here applied to Jesus; the fact that it is applied by believers means that it is perfectly right as far as it goes, but the fact that the believers are half-heathen Samaritans shows that it is only a very partial apprehension of the true character of the divine Logos which it is the purpose of the Gospel to expound.

There is no book in the N.T. which has suffered so much

---

[1] For this expectation cf. Wendland in *Zeitschr. f. d. N.T. Wiss.* 5 (1904), 335 f. and Nock in *Essays on the Trinity and the Incarnation* (ed. Rawlinson, 87 ff.).

[2] Phil. 3. 20, where he is trying to adapt the eschatological tradition of primitive Christianity to the hellenistic idea of the Christian life as already lived in the immaterial heavenly world.

[3] Probably the resemblance is merely due to the fact that the writer is following a similar tradition of theology (for pagan references cf. p. 38, n. 1); but the coincidence shows the danger.

[4] Wendland, op. cit. 349 ff.

[5] Hoskyns and Davey (*The Fourth Gospel*, 1. 272) miss the point almost as much as Loisy whom they controvert. That Jesus has delivered us from the present evil age is of course a commonplace of Christian writers from the beginning; the point is that the writer uses a title with such pagan associations and puts it into the mouth of the half-heathen Samaritan converts. The interpolation 'the Christ' here (for the MS. evidence cf. *The Fourth Gospel*, loc. cit.) dates from a period when Christian piety had forgotten that Jesus was the Messiah of Israel, not the Saviour of the cosmos.

from the conventional dichotomy of Judaism into Palestinian and Hellenistic as this Gospel. It is written in singularly poor Greek with a very limited vocabulary; the peculiarities of the Greek suggest that the writer was at least more at home in Aramaic.[1] Hence it has been argued that, since the writer knows little Greek, he cannot have been influenced by Greek ideas.[2] And so it is held that we have a document produced by an early stage of Palestinian Christianity, with high claims to be regarded as the story of an eyewitness of the earthly life of Jesus. For some unexplained reason the writer identified Jesus with the rather shadowy Memra or word of God which plays a somewhat unimportant role in the Targums as a periphrasis for the divine name.[3] Now it is perfectly possible that the Memra once played a much larger part in Jewish speculation than the extant Jewish literature suggests, and that rabbinical Judaism was once quite prepared to speculate about a Memra-Logos. We know singularly little about Judaism before the codification of the Mishnah after the fall of Jerusalem. What is certain is that such speculations, if they existed, were due to hellenistic influence. In the Fourth Gospel Jesus as the Logos fulfils the same function as the Logos of Philo, and a large part of the Gospel is devoted to an exposition of His life and work in terms of the same allegorical symbolism as that which Philo habitually employs, and reads into that symbolism the same conventional conceptions of theistic philosophy.

[1] Burney's thesis (*Aramaic Origin of the Fourth Gospel*) that it is translated from an Aramaic original has failed to win general acceptance, cf. W. E. Barnes in *J.T.S.* 23. 419 ff., and Colwell, *The Greek of the Fourth Gospel* (Chicago, 1931). On the other hand, some explanation of the writer's poor Greek and limited vocabulary is required; he is not an almost illiterate simpleton but an artist of a high order. The most natural explanation is that he was more at home in Aramaic than in Greek. But this does not prove that he was John the son of Zebedee or an eyewitness of the ministry of Jesus. There must have been a very large number of Christians in the first century A.D. who were more at home in Aramaic than in Greek; it is quite possible that they formed a majority of the Church.

[2] Schlatter, *Der Evangelist Johannes*, viii.

[3] Cf. Burney, op. cit. 38; for the relative unimportance of the Memra in the Targums (it does not appear elsewhere in rabbinical literature) cf. Moore, 'Intermediaries in Jewish Theology', *H.T.R.* 15 (1922), 41, and *Judaism*, 1. 416. For references to the Memra cf. Str.-B. 2. 306 and 313 ff. Cf. also Streeter, *The Four Gospels*[5], 374 ff. It is a weakness in Moore's position that he does not allow for the possibility that the Judaism of the first century A.D. may have differed considerably from that of the Talmud in view of the inevitable reaction against speculations which might be taken to support Christianity.

On the other hand, nothing could be more fantastic than to suppose that the writer of the Fourth Gospel had read Philo's works and deliberately substituted the figure of Jesus for the Philonic Logos. It would be inconceivable that the freshness and spontaneity of the Gospel were derived from the laborious pedantry of Philo. But the resemblance between them is easy to understand if both are drawing on a common stock of midrashic tradition, intended in the first instance to prove that the imagery of the O.T., if properly understood, revealed beneath a cloak of allegory the truths at which the great thinkers of Greece had only guessed and so to convert the Greeks or to preserve the educated Jew from apostasy. The Fourth Gospel uses the same imagery to prove that Jesus is the Logos of Greek philosophy manifested on the stage of history.[1] But the author derived both his imagery and his not very extensive philosophy not from the pages of Philo but from the general tradition of the schools in which the Jew was trained to commend his faith to the Gentile; it is at least possible that when he learnt that tradition it had been translated from Greek into Aramaic. In any case, he is like St. Paul the product of the mixed Greek-Jewish culture of the first century A.D. But this culture was to be found anywhere in the Jewish world and was taken over by the growing Christian culture of which St. Paul is the first literary representative.

For it is from the specifically Christian tradition that his choice of the Gospel-form for the delivery of his message is derived. Jewish writers and speakers were accustomed to use an historical summary of the Old Testament narrative as a means of exposition, selecting incidents which would support the view they were concerned to maintain and accompanying them if necessary with a running commentary.[2] The evangelist might have expounded his message in the form of a series of tracts (perhaps thrown into the form of letters) in which he explained his conception of the person and work of Jesus in terms of the

[1] Hoskyns and Davey, *The Fourth Gospel*, 158, object to this interpretation of the Logos of the Fourth Gospel on the ground that 'Jesus is also the Truth, the Light, the Life, the Way, the Resurrection, the Door. He is also the Bread from heaven.' But as will be seen below the Logos of Philo is also the Truth, the Light, the Life, and the Bread from heaven; he is also the Living Water, the Vine, and the Shepherd. It is possible that if we had more of this Jewish-hellenistic literature we should find that he can be the Way (cf. III, p. 78, n. 2 for an approximation to this) and the Door; but these may have been taken over from the Synoptic tradition.

[2] Cf. *Gentiles*, 28 and 123.

various images which he has selected for the purpose. His choice of the Gospel-form seems to have been dictated by the fact that it was already when he wrote the recognized method of expounding the kerygma of Christianity, and that the form was so firmly fixed that it could not be abandoned.[1]

The result is a work which appears to stand independently as a record of the life and teaching of Jesus, but really implies throughout a knowledge of the synoptic tradition in the reader, and employs so much of it as is necessary in order to make a Gospel. A further element in it consists of controversies with the Jews which may in some cases go back to good tradition and sometimes reflect a knowledge of rabbinical methods of argument. There is, however, no reason for supposing that such methods could not be learnt in the synagogues of Antioch and Ephesus, and in fact the controversies normally reveal themselves as controversies between the Church and the synagogue rather than between Jesus and the Jews.[2]

With these elements we are not primarily concerned; they are the common property of early Christianity. Our concern will be with the author's use of his remarkable skill as a story-

---

[1] For the relation of the Fourth Gospel to the synoptic writers cf. Streeter, *The Four Gospels*, 395 ff. He holds that John used Mark and Luke. Gardner-Smith (*St. John and the Synoptic Gospels*) argues from differences of meaning and setting in passages common to the Fourth Gospel and one or more of the others that he did not know our Gospel but an independent oral tradition, similar to that lying behind Mark but differing in detail. His view rests on the claim that many of the differences have no symbolic value; but it is always possible that some of the changes were once intended to have such a value, but that it is now lost. In any case, it would seem that the use of the form of a Gospel is dictated by the fact that it is recognized as the correct method of expounding the meaning of the life and work of Jesus. It is perfectly possible that there were several cycles of oral tradition apart from those which have survived in the Synoptic Gospels, dealing quite largely with the same events but differing in wording, and that such a cycle, which was never written down (or was soon lost), is the source of the Fourth Gospel's narrative.

[2] Cf. below, pp. 45, 65, &c. For the hidden Messiah of 7. 27 (cf. Rev. 12. 5 and Charles in *I.C.C.*, ad loc.) cf. Justin, Dial. 8. 226 b; his form of the belief is implied in Jno. 1. 31. It is clear from Justin that this belief was not specifically 'Palestinian'. The rabbinical argument in 10. 34 deals with an obvious difficulty; for rabbinical solutions cf. Hoskyns and Davey, ad loc. But similar difficulties were common to Judaism anywhere; cf. Philo's explanation of Exod. 7. 1 in Leg. Alleg. 1. 40 and De Sacr. Ab. et Cain. 9 and *passim*.

For the view that the arguments with the Jews represent the conflicts of the Church and the synagogue cf. R. H. Strachan, *The Fourth Gospel*, 23.

teller[1] in order to expound in the form of a Gospel the Pauline identification of Jesus with the divine Wisdom-Logos through the medium of the conventional symbolism of hellenistic Judaism.[2] It is not to be supposed that the author was conscious that he was changing the Gospel any more than the midrashic exponents of the O.T. were conscious of changing the sacred story. Since the Torah was God's revelation of Himself to Israel, anything that glorified the Torah or Israel must also glorify God, whether it happened to be true or not. In the same way the evangelist assumes that it is legitimate to rewrite the Gospel in order to bring out its theological meaning. He is conscious that in doing so he is writing something which can almost claim to be holy Scripture, introducing into the Church a work which the reader must interpret by finding out the allegorical meaning which

[1] Cf. Holtzmann, *Das Johannesevangelium*, 116; Scott, *The Fourth Gospel*, 18 ff. The use of short dramatic passages, which leave everything to the reader's imagination (13. 30, 18. 27 and 40, 19. 22), is amazingly effective from the narrative point of view; the commentators do not quote any parallels from ancient literature. Their real purpose is to call attention to the symbolical meaning (cf. Orig. in Joann. 32. 24 for 13. 30; for 18. 27 Strachan, op. cit. 271; 19. 35 is a note to bring out the meaning of v. 34). It seems that the evangelist hit on this method by reversing the normal method of allegory; instead of an elaborate explanation of an inspired sentence he writes a single sentence, which it is left to others to understand and expound. This implies that he is consciously writing more or less inspired literature (cf. Windisch, *Unt. z. N.T.* 12 (1926); *Joh. u. d. Synoptiker*, 149) in which a striking sentence is always a mark of deep symbolical meaning (cf. Philo, De Post Cain. 7).

[2] There is a certain parallel in the treatment of the story of Genesis and Exodus as an aretalogy of Wisdom in Wisd. 10, and in the Jewish-Stoic document preserved under a Christian veneer in the liturgy of the Apostolic Constitutions, 7. 33. 1 ff.; here in 34. 1 Wisdom probably held the place now given to Christ, as also in 36. 1. In 35. 10 we have a duplication of God as Father of Wisdom and of Christ. In the parallel version 8. 12. 9 ff. God discusses creation with Wisdom as He does with the Logos in Philo (*Gentiles*, 83, n. 1). For the whole cf. Bousset in *Gött. gel. Nachr.* 1915, 435 ff. In these documents there is no serious change in the canonical story; but for the extent to which that story could be altered in the interests of piety cf. Jos. Antt. 1. 155 f. (Abraham) and the Jewish writers *ap.* Eus. Pr. Ev. 9. 14 ff.; Philo, De Abr. 69 f., and De Vit. Moys. 1. 25 ff. (modelled on Nicholas of Damascus' life of Augustus, Jacoby, *F.G.H.* 2 a. 391, or on a pattern common to both). In the Fourth Gospel we have the established kerygma of the story of Jesus set forth as the story of the manifestation of the Logos, as against the story of creation or the Exodus, treated with a freedom similar to that of the writings referred to. There is of course an immeasurable difference in the interest of the story concerned and in the literary skill of the evangelist as against the Jewish writers.

lies beneath his symbolism in order to understand the fullness of the life of Jesus as the theophany of the Logos.

NOTE

Philo's Use of Sources

Apart from the 'secular' source isolated by Bousset [*Jüd.-Christl. Schulbetrieb in Alexandria u. Rom*, 43 ff.], various philosophical tracts are incorporated more or less wholesale at various points in Philo's writings, as in De Plant. 142 ff. [cf. v. Arnim, *Quellenstudien zu Philo*, 101 ff.]. Various other such incorporations, together with the literature on the subject, are noted by Cohn–Wendland in their edition of the text, while Stein in 'Die Allegorische Exegese des Philo' and 'Philo u. d. Midrasch' (*Ztschr. f. d. A.T. Wissenschaft*, 1928/9 (51) and 1931/2 (57) has made some valuable, but still only preliminary, attempts to clear up the lines on which the problem of Philo's sources should be approached.[1] I give here some further specimens of Philo's methods of compilation.

(1) De Mund. Op. 89–127. It is possible that a large part of this treatise incorporates a cosmogony of Posidonius, based on the Timaeus. This section is a panegyric on the virtue of the hebdomad, as exemplified by God's rest on the seventh day and the Jewish sabbath, a theme which goes back to Aristobulus (Eus. Pr. Ev. 13. 12. 15) and is intended to prove that Pythagoras bears witness to the truth of Judaism. We have the usual play with numbers and the usual dissertation on the importance of the hebdomad in the cosmos and in man the microcosm. In the course of it we learn that 'other philosophers' compare it to the Virgin Victory which sprang fully armed from the head of Zeus, the Pythagoreans to the ruler of all things. The argument is supported by quotations from Solon, Hippocrates (twice), Plato, and Philolaus (in striking contrast to Philo's normal method of quoting classical authors[2]), and the Latin tongue which marks the σεμνότης of the number by adding 'S' to ἑπτά to make it 'septem' (Philo makes no other allusion to the Latin language). In the whole of the argument there is no allusion to Judaism or the O.T. after 89; if the clause which connects 128 with what precedes it (ταῦτα καί . . . ἀνωτάτω) be omitted, the rest of the section could stand by itself as a continuation of 89. On the other hand, we have an allusion to pagan mythology which conveys no hint of reprobation and a wealth of allusions to pagan writers. Much of the medical and astronomical lore and the quotation from Solon recurs in Clement of Alexandria (Strom. 6. 16. 145, 815 P.), who seems to have derived it from Hermippus of Berytus, a pupil of Philo of Byblos whose

---

[1] I am indebted to my friend Dr. W. J. Gutbrod of Tübingen for drawing my attention to these two articles.

[2] For Philo's treatment of classical writers see below, p. 53.

date appears to be *c.* A.D. 150 (P.W.K., s.v. 'Hermippus'). But the theme and method of treatment goes back at least to Varro; a similar and largely identical elaboration of the merits of the hebdomad from his pen is preserved by Aulus Gellius (Noct. Att. 3. 10. 1 ff.). It is quite unthinkable that a pious Jew could have composed a panegyric on the hebdomad which included a comparison of it to the Virgin Victory which sprang fully armed from the head of Zeus; it is remarkable that he should have left it unrevised.

(2) There is, however, a more remarkable instance. In Leg. ad G. we begin a glowing account of the joy which hailed the accession of Caligula; it made the stories of the reign of Cronos seem not a myth but a present reality (8 ff.). Soon after his accession he fell ill; the world's joy at his recovery seemed like the emergence of mankind from barbarism to civilization. Then his deterioration set in and we read of his crimes. They are followed by a satire, modelled on such passages as Isocrates, Busiris, 11. 7, on his attempt to represent himself as such demigods as Heracles, the cleanser of the world from evil, Dionysus, the bringer of gladness to man, or the Dioscuri, famed for their mutual love. Caligula was their exact opposite. But he went further and sought to win the veneration of the greater gods who are divine on both sides; he represented himself as Hermes, the bringer of good news, whereas he was associated with nothing but evil tidings; as Apollo the healer of mankind, whereas he was their destroyer; as Ares, but the true Ares, as opposed to the mythical, is the Logos in nature which has peace for its province, the power which watches over the oppressed and establishes peace. Hence he could not claim to resemble any god (§ 114). 'But it seems that desire is blind, especially when it is joined to vainglory and ambition, coupled with supreme authority; and it was by this that we, who formerly were happy, were ravaged, for he persecuted the Jews alone.' Bousset (op. cit. 148) defends the passage as Philo's *reductio ad absurdum* of Caligula's apotheosis of himself. It may be admitted that in the De Providentia (2. 41, A. 76) he uses the common Stoic explanation of polytheism and apparently immoral mythology, that the gods are symbols of the elements and forces of nature; but there, as Bousset rightly notes (loc. cit.), he is simply copying a Stoic tract on providence. I find it quite unthinkable that a pious Jew should have written in the style of this passage instead of denouncing the blasphemy involved in a man's representing himself as God, as in De Post. Cain. 115. Naturally Jews had to be careful about denouncing the imperial cult, but elsewhere in this tract (118 and 138 ff.) the Jewish view is clearly expressed. It would seem that Philo has once again incorporated a pagan source without troubling to correct it; the document would seem to be an Alexandrine lampoon in the Stoic vein, ridiculing Caligula's attempt to represent himself as a God; whether it was compiled after his assassination or circulated secretly before it does not appear. (For the Alexandrine opposition to

the Empire and attacks of this kind cf. Wilcken and Premerstein, op. cit. p. 11, n. 4).

It may be noticed that a further section, 141–51, comes from the same or a similar source, with 148 inserted to adapt it to the peculiar case of the Jewish synagogues.[1] To suppose that a devout Jew could sit down to write a panegyric on the splendour of the Temple of Augustus and its images is entirely ludicrous.

(3) Philo's treatment of the names of God reveals a similar use of sources. Generally he follows the halakha of the Mishnah; the Name may only be uttered by those who are pure in the holy place, i.e. as part of the Temple service. The Name is of four letters; this leads on to a characteristic account of the value of the tetrad (De Vit. Moys. 2 (3). 114 ff.). Shortly after in his account of the High Priest's robe (ib. 132 ff.) we read that on the mitre are the four letters of which 'they say' the Name is composed. There is a variant 'he says' (i.e. Moses), but this looks like an attempt to avoid the obvious difficulty that Philo, who has quite recently said that the Name is of four letters, should now write that 'they say' it is of four letters. Philo goes on to expound the symbolism of the robe; the robe symbolizes the cosmos, and the true worshipper must be 'if it be right to say so—and it is right not to lie when one is speaking of the truth—a little cosmos'. The symbolism of the robe is a commonplace of hellenistic Judaism, and Philo reverts to it elsewhere (De Migr. Abr. 103 f.). In this passage it would seem that Philo has put together a short tract on the symbolism of the robe (109–16) and a longer one (117–35), the former of which was better informed than the latter as to the writing on the mitre; the symbolism read into the Name differs completely; in 115 it deals with the virtues of the tetrad, in 132 with the name of Jahveh as 'He who is'. In any case the latter of the two is not Philo's own composition in the first instance. For the closing sentence of 135 apologizes for the use of the macrocosm-microcosm analogy with the words 'if it be right to say so'. But in fact it is one of Philo's favourite platitudes, while the tract itself is regarded as one of Philo's later ones (Bréhier and Massebiau, Rev. de l'Hist. des Rel., Jan.–June 1906, 34 ff.). In any case the former of the two preserves the tradition of the Mishnah that the Name may only be uttered in the Temple service (Mishnah, Yôma 6. 2, Sotah 7. 6, Danby, pp. 169 and 301).

But in Leg. ad G. 353 Caligula insults the Jewish envoys by referring to their unnameable God and then uttering 'the name, which it is not lawful to hear, much less to pronounce'. Philo's statement that

---

[1] Note the elaborate οὖτός ἐστιν ὁ of 145 ff., and cf. p. 70, n. 1, for this style of oratory; Philo could, of course, use the style, but he could not have written 150 f.

It is of interest that Ares in 112 is a logos in nature possessing a δύναμις of helping the wronged and establishing peace; the reference should be added to those in Gentiles, 50, n. 1, for the source of the 'powers' in Philo.

it is not lawful to hear it, much less to pronounce it, is quite inconsistent with the statement of De Vit. Moys. 2 (3). 114, that it may only be heard and uttered by the High Priest in the Temple. This might be ascribed to mere slovenliness on Philo's part, but for the fact that Philo's language here is in accordance with the statement that when the High Priest uttered the Name, the attendant priests drowned it with their singing, while the High Priest only uttered it in a low voice (*Judaism*, 1. 425; the statement goes back to R. Tarphon). But elsewhere (De Decal. 93) Philo preserves an entirely different halakha, to the effect that a man who swears an oath must be pure in body (i.e. ritually), soul, and tongue; for it is not right that a mouth which utters the most holy Name should also utter anything shameful. (For this older practice and its abandonment cf. Str.-B. on Mt. 5. 34, 3 a, p. 330 f.) Here then we have three distinct stages of Jewish practice, but Philo nowhere suggests that there has been a change in the rule during his lifetime. On the other hand, Caligula's knowledge of the Mishnaic prohibition implies that it had been in force for a considerable period; he could not have known it unless it was a matter of common knowledge; the actual name Iao was of course well known in the Greek world, and the fact that the Jews had ceased to pronounce it would take some time to gain general publicity. It is very difficult to avoid the conclusion that the earliest stage, represented by De Decal., is taken from a source which is older than Philo's own lifetime. It might of course be argued that on so trivial a matter Philo cannot be expected to be consistent; but to a Jew of this first century A.D. the matter was one which, rightly or wrongly, seemed of vast importance.

(4) Philo's treatment of allegory as a method of interpreting the O.T. reveals a contradiction which is at least highly suspicious. In De Conf. Ling. 14 he leaves the defence of the literal meaning of the story of the Tower of Babel to those whose business it is to explain away any difficulties that the text may seem to raise. These literal exegetes, who include the whole body of rabbinical teachers, are mentioned with the utmost respect. On the other hand, in De Somn. 1. 102 after ridiculing the command as to the debtor's cloak in Exod. 22. 26 f., he concludes by saying, 'Let this be our answer to the sophists of the literal interpretation and the ultra-highbrows (τοὺς λίαν τὰς ὀφρῦς ἀνεσπακότας), but let us follow the laws of allegory and say what is fitting on these matters'. Probably Philo's own view is that laid down in De Migr. Abr. 89, that we must both seek out the allegorical meaning and observe the letter. It might be argued that in De Somn. we have merely an incidental inconsistency, due to the necessity of explaining away the debtor's cloak (cf. 1 Cor. 9. 9). But this does not explain the lengthy tirade of De Somn. 1. 92 ff., which shows that the whole question was one of lively controversy. As a matter of fact the whole passage up to 112 comes from a source (Bousset's 'secular source') which is concerned to vindicate the study of

philosophy for Judaism (the creditor who does not restore the cloak, which symbolizes reason, = the teacher who keeps the soul in lower studies), to which Philo has added a totally irrelevant and inconsistent fragment of piety, to the effect that we must restore the Logos to its proper place in the soul, while God still causes His light to shine on us; otherwise we shall be condemned to a perpetuity of darkness like the Egyptians when they sought to detain Israel.

(5) Philo's use of O.T. sources. I have dealt with this in *J.T.S.* 41. 161. 30 ff. A criticism of this article from the late Mr. F. H. Colson appeared in the same journal (41. 163–4. 237 ff.).[1] His criticisms, however, do not in any way affect the main facts, namely that Philo's use of the O.T. for the most part ignores all but the Pentateuch. This is all the more remarkable when it is remembered how much such favourite Philonic themes as the creation of the world and the attributes of God are associated by the rabbis with the book of Job, which Philo quotes once (De Mut. Nom. 48) with no reference to cosmogony, and with Ezekiel's chapter of the chariot, which he ignores entirely. Further the quotations (some fifty in all) tend to come not singly but in groups of two or three fairly close together, while twenty of the number deal with two particular themes, the divine Wisdom and the birth of Samuel,[2] in which Hannah represents mystical contemplation, two themes which Philo associates in Q.D.S.I. 5, where Hannah as grace is the gift of the divine Wisdom. It must be remembered that both mystical contemplation and the concept of the cosmic Wisdom represent matters in which Judaism is open to the suspicion of having borrowed from the religion of Egypt; and if an O.T. justification for mystical contemplation was to be found, it was hardly possible to find it except in Hannah (1 Sam. 1. 13; it is very doubtful if there is any other case in which we are told so definitely that prayers were not uttered with the lips). If the Hannah-Samuel-Wisdom group of testimonies and the grouped quotations be omitted we are left with twenty quotations from outside the Pentateuch

[1] No student of Philo can be unaware of the debt he owes to Mr. Colson or of the temerity of disagreeing with him. It seemed more courteous to his memory to leave my reply to his criticisms (written before his death) to stand, rather than to ignore them.

[2] Mr. Colson objected that it is natural that Samuel as one of the most impressive O.T. figures outside the Pentateuch should figure so largely. This misses the point. Samuel normally appears as the type of the 'seer' who represents the mystical vision of God, which is the child of Hannah, i.e. the result of a divine gift of Grace. His history is ignored except in De Migr. Abr. 196 (a passage in which wisdom appears as a kingdom; the reference is to the Stoic view of the wise man, but for the confusion of the cosmic Wisdom of Proverbs with the Stoic cf. Wisd. 6. 12 ff.). Yet what a store of allegorical platitudes could have been derived from the hewing of Agag in pieces before the Lord as a proof of the need of extirpating vice from the soul! The other passages deal entirely with his birth and his description as a 'seer'.

(two of them repeated twice). Even so we have not come to the end of the peculiarities, since apart from a group of three in De Conf. Ling. 39–52 we have four isolated quotations (Mr. Colson objected to treating the three as a group; if his objection be admitted, we have five isolated quotations and a group of two in one tract); in De Mut. Nom. we have five, four in the main midrash and one in the long interpolated section 60–130 in which Philo replies to the ridicule of anti-semites who ask why there should be such a fuss over the change of name from Abram to Abraham and Sarai to Sarah, and incidentally avails himself of the interpolation to avoid the awkward mention of circumcision in Gen. 17. 10. The interpolated section is remarkable for the large number of names which are interpreted with a reasonable knowledge of Hebrew as against the general ignorance of Hebrew which Philo displays.[1]

I suggested in J.T.S., loc. cit. 34, that the probable explanation of this curious absence of quotations from outside the Pentateuch in the greater part of Philo's writings, and their relative frequency in these two tracts and in the sections where we find the groups of quotations (there are three such groups in Q.D.S.I.), is that for the most part Philo is incorporating the midrashic tradition of Alexandria as it was developed at a period when the Pentateuch alone was translated into Greek. The Wisdom testimonies would seem to go back to Philo's predecessors, since Wisdom in Philo is merely a duplicate of the Logos, which is tending to oust the earlier cosmic figure. It would be tempting to conjecture that Hannah and Samuel reflect the interest of Philo's 'therapeutae' in contemplative prayer, if it were certain that they had any historical existence,[2] but in any case such types would be needed to justify the practice of mystical prayer in orthodox Judaism. These quotations, as Mr. Colson pointed out, presuppose a knowledge of the LXX in De Ebr. 149; it would seem that they also included testimonies

---

[1] Reuben, Symeon, Ephraim, Manasseh (a different interpretation from Gen. 41. 51, but reasonably possible), Raguel, Beelphegor, Phineas (apparently פה נחש 'interpreting mouth' represented by τρανός), Zipporah (as a bird suitable as a symbol of inspired prophecy), Hosea הו זה (= this is he that = this is the kind of man that), Caleb. Of these 10 only 3 appear elsewhere in Philo. For Philo's general ignorance of Hebrew cf. Stein, Alleg. Exeg. 20 ff.

[2] It is significant that Philo does not know whence his therapeutae derived their names (De Vit. Cont. 2). But there were therapeutae attached to Egyptian temples (cf. Cumont, L'Ég. des Astrol. 147 f.). They go back at least to Ptolemaic times. Philo's Jewish therapeutae are extremely suspicious; they may very well be invented in order to prove that Judaism has its therapeutae no less than the Gentiles. In any case it seems probable that if they really existed they were imitated from the devotees of paganism; since Judaism had no temple in Egypt (that of Onias hardly catered for this type of Judaism, and it is in any case ignored by Philo and his orthodox sources), they would have to be living in houses of their own (near the Mareotic lake).

for use against the Gentiles, the quotation of Hesiod (Works and Days 287 ff.) being used to justify the practice of asceticism as necessary for the soul which seeks to attain to contemplation (here = virtue as in De Vit. Cont. 90). They would appear therefore to be later than Philo's other sources, but to go back beyond Philo himself, if Hannah was originally associated with Wisdom; but it is of course possible that Philo is himself responsible for connecting them and that the connexion of Hannah with Wisdom in Q.D.S.I. 5 is merely an *obiter dictum* of Philo himself.

It must be remembered that Philo's peculiar method of writing in which an O.T. text leads to a rambling disquisition, in which verbal association plays at least as large a part as continuity of thought, ending in a return to the text which follows, is not Philonic but characteristic of Jewish haggada, as is also the habit of repeating the same passage with little or no change wherever it seems to come in appropriately. In these peculiarities we simply have the ordinary lack of style or coherence characteristic of Jewish writing. The difference is that in rabbinical literature it is normal for the rabbis responsible for peculiarly striking views to be quoted by name, whereas Philo never does so. On the other hand, it must be remembered that Philo hoped for Greek readers, who would not be in the least impressed by the views of barbarian rabbis. But it is also to be observed that he treats Greek writers in the same way. Apart from the doxographic matter in De Aet. Mund. and De Providentia (note especially 1. 22) and the typical collection of anecdotes in 2. 5 ff. and in Q.O.P.L. we have a large number of references to pagan writers in De Mund. Op. 89–127 which has already been noticed as quite incompatible with Philo's whole outlook on paganism. Just after this section there is a reference to Plato by name (op. cit. 133). Elsewhere allusions to him and quotations from him appear frequently, but he is nowhere mentioned by name. The same applies to all other Greek writers, except that Heraclitus is mentioned three times, twice to be accused of borrowing from Moses (Leg. Alleg. 1. 108 and Q.R.D.H. 214), once to be condemned for his doctrine of flux (Leg. Alleg. 3. 7). Protagoras is mentioned by name in De Post. Cain. 35, but the name might easily have been inserted by a scholiast and found its way into the text. In view of this excision of Greek names (possibly in deference to Jewish readers) it is not unnatural that Jewish names should be omitted in deference to Greek readers; in any case we have no means of knowing how far the rabbinical practice of preserving the names of rabbis responsible for particular sayings was current in Alexandria.[1]

---

[1] It is at least possible that the rabbinical practice arose in the period before the codification of the Mishnah and during the growth of the Pharisaic movement, when it was necessary in the case of particular halakha to make it clear whose authority lay behind any particular view, and that it passed thence into haggadic writing. We do not know how far Pharisaism affected Alexandrine Judaism.

Philo's style does indeed show a remarkable uniformity. It is of course possible that this reflects the general tradition of fine writing and pulpit rhetoric current in educated Alexandrine Judaism. On the other hand, it is perfectly conceivable that Philo rewrote his sources fairly completely, though if this be the case it is remarkable that he should have failed to eliminate the obvious paganisms noted above in two particular tracts. Professor A. D. Nock in a private letter compares Diodorus Siculus, who has incorporated a number of sources, but reduces them to a general uniformity of style.

LECTURE III

THE thesis of the Fourth Gospel is stated in the prologue, which is a restatement of Mark 1. 1,[1] or a similar account of the ministry of Jesus in terms of Genesis 1. 1; but it is Genesis 1. 1 as interpreted in the light of the Wisdom-tradition of Proverbs 8. 22.[2] The interpretation of Genesis in this sense was familiar to rabbinical Judaism, which had taken it over from the hellenistic synagogues. Formally it is a cosmogony of a popular type, ultimately derived from the Timaeus of Plato, but already established as a conventional form of religious and missionary propaganda.[3] The language in which the Logos is described as life and light is a regular feature of the same tradition[4]; after all they are pre-eminently suited to describe the nature of God. The light had always shone in the darkness, but the darkness had never succeeded in understanding the light.[5]

[1] The intrusion of the Baptist in v. 6 breaks the sequence of the prologue; we do not really come to him till v. 15. He is, however, introduced here because the evangelist is concerned to correct Mk. 1. 1 (or a similar version of the Gospel) which made the appearance of the Baptist 'the beginning'.

[2] For the association of Gen. 1. 1 and Prov. 8. 22 in rabbinical literature cf. *Gentiles*, 113; Prov. 8. 22 and similar allusions to the cosmic Wisdom form a large part of Philo's O.T. references outside the Pentateuch, cf. Note on Lecture II above. In the extant rabbinical literature Wisdom at creation is simply a glorification of the Torah; her original purpose of reconciling Judaism with Greek thought has been forgotten.

[3] Philo's De Mundi Opificio is the most obvious specimen of this type. The Poimandres appears to conflate two such cosmogonies (Corp. Herm. 1. 5 a and 12 seem to be duplicates). The cosmic Wisdom makes an interesting appearance in Aristides' hymn to Sarapis (Or. 45 (8). 17, Keil, 2. 357), where she replaces Isis as teacher of religion, civilization, &c., apparently because a colourless Wisdom is not, as Isis, whom we should naturally expect here, might be, a dangerous rival to Sarapis (cf. Höfler, 'D. Sar. Hymn. d. Ail. Arist.', *Tübinger Beitr. z. Alt. Wiss.* 23–5 (1935), 5. 53). For other specimens cf. Clem. Alex. Exc. ex Theod. 7. 1 (Casey, 44. 62 ff.) adapted to the Fourth Gospel, the Naassene of Hipp. El. 5. 6. 4 ff., and the Gnostic cosmogonies in general. An elaborate specimen is the Ps. Arist. De Mundo 6. 1 ff.

[4] Cf. Philo, De Mund. Op. 30; Corp. Herm. 1. 9 and 21. For the Logos as light cf. Philo, De Somn. 1. 75, and the Stoic-Persian cosmogony of Dio Chrys. Or. 36. 55, where mind proceeds from God to create and at the end of each world-period resumes τὴν καθαρωτάτην αὐγῆς ἀκηράτου φύσιν (cf. Cumont, *Mag. Hell.* 1. 91; cf. also Aristides, loc. cit.).

[5] For καταλαμβάνειν of understanding God cf. *Gentiles*, 192. Schlatter, *Der Evangelist Johannes*, ad loc., holds that John always uses the word as = seize; but the Gospel only uses it three times. Hoskyns and Davey may be right in holding that there is a play on the two meanings of the word. But this implies that the evangelist was acquainted with a myth of the 'seizing' of

Thus in spite of the ministry of John as the witness of the light, the true light was rejected when it came into the world. Just as the cosmos which the light had created never knew Him,[1] so, when He came, the people He had chosen rejected Him. It is a regular feature of this type of cosmogony that the 'light' should be associated with 'truth',[2] which is again a natural description of God, perhaps inspired by the tradition of Zoroastrianism, but long since acclimatized in the Hellenistic world; it is no less characteristic of the lack of clarity of thought in this literature that in v. 12 the Logos should give to those who believed on Him the power to become the sons of God,[3] but

the light by the darkness as in Satornilus (Ir. Haer. 1. 18. 1) and preeminently in Manichaeism (cf. Polotzky in P.W.K. *Suppl.* vi. 251). It is possible that Philo's queer explanation of morning and evening in Genesis as barriers to keep light and darkness from conflict (De Mund. Op. 33) implies such a myth; but otherwise we have no proof that it goes back as far as the Fourth Gospel.

[1] 'The true light was always coming into the world' seems the only translation that gives any adequate meaning here. The continued action of the Light on the cosmos probably meant for the evangelist the opportunity which all men had of knowing the truth; but the parallels suggest that the cosmic activity of the Logos-light as immanent in the world *qua* cosmos has been changed into the activity of the Logos on the cosmos as consisting of mankind as cut off from God. For such activity cf. Aristides, op. cit. 18 ff., where Sarapis ἐκ μὲν θεῶν οἴκων οὐδὲ ἐξέρχεται, yet διὰ παντὸς ἡμῶν εἰσι τοῦ βίου and τὸ πᾶν πεπλήρωκε). Bauer, ad loc., quotes Mandean parallels and states that Philo holds that the Logos remains with God and does not go into the cosmos on the strength of Q.D.S.I. 31; this is true, but contrast De Sacr. Ab. et Cain. 67, De Plant. 9, Q.R.D.H. 188, De Fug. et Inv. 110 ff. For the Logos as light cf. De Somn. 1. 75.

[2] Bauer, ad loc., rightly interprets ἀληθινόν = 'full of truth' not simply 'genuine'. Cf. Aristides, 23 (42). 15, (K. 2. 35) τοῦ θεοῦ καλοῦντός τε ὡς αὐτὸν καὶ μαλὰ ἀληθινὸν φῶς ἀνίσχοντος and Celsus' use of ὦ φῶς καὶ ἀλήθεια in the sense of 'good God!' (Orig. c. Cels. 2. 49; Philo, Q.D.S.I. 96, Leg. Alleg. 3. 45, De Jos. 68, De Fug. et Inv. 139, where the manna = the divine ῥῆμα or Logos which enlightens the soul with the light of the truth. Cf. also Porphyry, Vit. Pyth. 41 of Ahura Mazda ἐοικέναι τὸ μὲν σῶμα φωτί, τὴν δὲ ψυχὴν ἀληθείᾳ and Anrich, *Ant. Myst.-Wesen*, 33, for the interpretation of the lights used in various cults as symbols of the illumination of the mind by truth. Cf. also Cumont, *Mag. Hell.* 2. 73, n. 5.

[3] The divine birth is properly the prerogative of kings (Cumont, *L'Ég. des Astr.* 26). For the inconsistency of the text cf. Dio Chrys. 4. 27: Zeus gives the knowledge of the art of kingship to whom he will, and those to whom he gives it are called and are the sons of Zeus. Cf. De Conf. Ling. 147 ff.: if we are not good enough to be counted sons of God. we must try to be worthy to be counted sons of His Logos. In De Conf. Ling. 77 the souls of the wise are temporary sojourners on earth, and are thus presumably of a special order of nobility; but normally nobility is simply attained by

that their power to receive Him should rest on the fact that they were already possessors of a divine birth.[1]

The cosmogony concludes with the appearance of the Logos in the flesh making His tabernacle among men. The term σκῆνος was normally associated with the pessimistic view of the material world in which the body was the tabernacle of a divine spark,[2] imprisoned in matter as a result of a celestial fall; here the evangelist treats the flesh and the σκῆνος as the medium of a divine revelation. He is perhaps assisted by the Jewish conception of the Shekhinah as dwelling among men,[3] but still more by his complete indifference to the philosophy whose language he borrows. The optimistic tradition of Stoicism was familiar with the thought that the cosmos or the Logos which animated it was the only-begotten son of God,[4] a thought which went back to the Timaeus; but the evangelist's language is largely borrowed from the pessimistic view which saw in the flesh and the material the source of evil.[5] At times he is capable of a dualism

virtue, as in the whole tract De Nobilitate. Judaism was in a peculiarly difficult position, since it could not be doubted that Israel was superior to other nations (cf. De Vit. Moys. 1. 279), but it had to be admitted that a good proselyte was better than a bad Israelite.

[1] The variant ὃς ἐγεννήθη implied in the Latin versions may be due to the desire to avoid the apparent inconsistency or to eliminate the Gnostic suggestion of the text, cf. Tert. De Carne Christi, 19 and 24.

[2] Wisd. 9. 15, 2 Cor. 5. 1, and cf. *Gentiles*, 137; for the fall of the spiritual man into the prison of the flesh cf. ib. 83.

[3] For the Shekhinah cf. *Judaism*, 1. 369 ff.; Rev. 21. 3. The Shekhinah is so much a commonplace of Judaism that it is fantastic to read into this passage a contrast between the flesh of Jesus and the Temple at Jerusalem, in which the evangelist takes no interest, except in so far as its destruction proves the end of the old dispensation.

[4] Cf. Timaeus 92 c for the cosmos as 'only begotten'. For the optimistic view of the cosmos cf. Philo, Q.R.D.H. 199, De Abr. 74, De Migr. Abr. 179, Corp. Herm. 5. 9, 8. 2. Ps.-Arist. De Mundo 6. 6, holds equally that the cosmos is very good, although the sublunar sphere is a kind of sediment at the bottom. Philo is of course quite capable of writing in the opposite vein for which the material is evil; in De Spec. Leg. 1. 329 God can only touch it through His powers; cf. De Post. Cain. 61. In De Jos. 145 we have the precise view of Ps.-Arist. above. Philo never makes the cosmos as such evil; but matter and flesh are normally so. In Corp. Herm. 9. 4 b we have perhaps a polemic against Christianity for making the cosmos as against the earth the home of evil; cf. Scott's note ad loc. and the list of vices in the Jewish-Christian fashion in 3. But the hermetic writings are inconsistent; in 6. 4 b the cosmos is far from perfect and in 13. 1 definitely evil; here perhaps we have Christian influence, cf. below, Note I on Regeneration.

[5] For the flesh as the source of evil cf. Philo, Q.D.S.I. 140 ff., and *Gentiles*, 83.

in which the material is as evil as it was to St. Paul; none the less 'flesh' could be assumed by the Logos for the simple reason that the evangelist is entirely clear that the historical Jesus was the revelation of God to the world and is entirely unconcerned with speculations as to the origin of evil.

The incarnation of the Logos in time brings us back to the problem of John. It might be supposed that as prior in time he was also greater than Jesus.[1] But this is ruled out by the testimony of John himself, who knew that he was only the last in a series of partial revelations which culminated in the full revelation of grace and truth in Jesus Christ.[2] Such a full revelation is entirely compatible with the dogma of philosophy that God Himself is invisible; for though God Himself cannot be seen His Logos can be manifested, normally in the cosmos but for the Christian in the flesh of the only-begotten Logos.[3]

[1] It is possible that the reference to the Baptist is a polemic against sects which regarded the Baptist as the Messiah, cf. Lohmeyer, *Das Urchristentum*, 1. 13 ff. But we have very little evidence for such sects, if once the Mandeans are abandoned (cf. Lietzmann, *Gesch. d. alt. Kirche*, 1. 33). It is doubtful whether the author's real purpose is not to prove that Jesus as the Messiah had really been preceded by Elijah in the person of John, cf. above Lecture II, p. 45, n. 2. For priority in time as implying superiority cf. Philo, De Mund. Op. 27.

[2] Grace here might come from the Hellenistic-Jewish tradition, cf. Q.D.S.I. 107, De Somn. 2. 183 where the Logos is the medium of God's graces. But in Philo at any rate 'grace' is usually used in the plural to cover natural as well as spiritual gifts, with the result that the concept is so wide as to have little real meaning; it seems probable that the evangelist is following the specifically Christian tradition derived from St. Paul. For v. 16 as meaning that the old dispensation was a partial and progressive bestowal of 'graces' cf. Büchsel in *T.W.z.N.T.* 1. 373, who quotes Philo, De Post. Cain. 145 which shows the kind of source on which the Gospel draws very clearly. Verse 17 seems to be the writer's comment on John's words, making it clear that he was the end of the old, not the beginning of the new dispensation.

[3] Verse 18 is added to make it clear that Christianity has not abandoned the claim of Judaism to have the true revelation of the 'invisible God' (cf. *Gentiles*, 45 ff., and add to references given there Strabo 10. 3. 9 (467), Athen. Leg. pro Christ. 10 (Schwartz, 10. 44 ff.)). Here the Logos as the visible manifestation of God replaces the cosmos; for Stoic thought it was a commonplace that God was easily seen as manifested in the cosmos, cf. *Gentiles*, 70. This confusion of the cosmos and the Logos appears in Philo, De Conf. Ling. 147, where if we cannot be sons of God, we must be sons of the Logos; this is Philo's own adaptation of the view that the suppliant, if he cannot be worthy of God, must be worthy of the cosmos, which he takes over from his source in De Vit. Moys. 2 (3). 135; cf. Corp. Herm. Ascl. 1. 8 (Scott, 298). Philo naturally holds that God is invisible, though

Such is the theme of the prologue; it is worked out in the Gospel in a series of episodes, which illustrate the main theme. In some of them indeed it plays little or no part; there seems to be no hint of it in the story of the nobleman's son at Capernaum; in the story of the call of the first disciples the synoptic tradition has been rewritten in order to reassert the claim that Jesus was superior to John in spite of the latter's priority in the order of time (1. 30); but the author takes the opportunity of pointing out that Jesus is not merely the Messiah foretold by Moses and the prophets (1. 45), whose power of reading men's thoughts at a distance proves Him to be the son of God and the king of Israel (1. 49), but also the Logos, who is the means of communication between God and man, seen by Jacob in his dream at Bethel but now to be manifested in all His glory. But this is scarcely more than an incidental allusion.[1] In one incident, the marriage at Cana, it seems that we have a heathen folk-tale,

He can be seen with the eyes of the mind; Israel is the soul or race that sees God (De Post. Cain. 63, De Conf. Ling. 92 and *passim*; cf. Corp. Herm. 4. 5, 5. 2.) But in De Somn. 1. 65 man cannot see God but only His Logos, while in De Mut. Nom. 8 man cannot see God but only the things that come after Him (the 'Hinder-parts' of Exod. 33. 23 apparently = the cosmos). The evangelist is thus verbally within the proprieties of philosophy in combining an invisible God with a visible 'first-born'. Naturally neither Judaism nor Christianity could accept divine immanence which would make the cosmos the visible manifestation of God. Bauer, ad loc., gives various parallels to μονογενής from Eastern religions, but ignores Plato Timaeus 92 c.

[1] Jacob's ladder is occasionally associated with the Messiah, cf. Str.–B. ad loc. But in Philo it symbolizes (1) the air, the home of disembodied souls; the passage De Somn. 1. 133 ff. recurs in a slightly different form in De Gig. 7 ff., and Cicero, De Nat. Deor. 2. 15. 42 ff., where the aether replaces Philo's absurd 'lower air' and proves the divinity of the stars not the existence of angels, who in any case ought to live in the aether (cf. Bousset, *Jud. chris. Schul-betr.* 14 ff.). (2) In De Somn. 1. 146 it also symbolizes the soul, through which in man the microcosm divine logoi pass, raising it up to the level of mind. By analogy it would follow that the ladder in the macrocosm is the divine Logos. Cosmic ladders appear in Aristides, Ἱεροὶ Λόγοι, 3. 48 (Keil, 2. 424), where he sees a ladder in a vision; it symbolizes the power of Sarapis both on earth and below. In Orig. c. Cels. 6. 22 we find a ladder symbolizing the ascent to the firmament, while, ib. 21, he claims that Jacob's vision proves that Moses anticipated Plato, Phaedr. 248 c ff. Cf. also Cumont, *After-life*, 153. The Son of Man here, who is continually kept in touch with the divine Logos by angels or divine logoi, replaces the Synoptic Son of Man coming with angels on the clouds of heaven. (Angels in this Gospel only here and in 20. 12 where they could not be eliminated from the tradition; possibly also in 5. 4 (for the text cf. Hoskyns and Davey ad loc.), but only in a very subordinate position taken over from Jewish tradition.)

which has somehow been attached to Jesus; it is used to reinforce the claim that Christianity is superior to Judaism, though
later in order of time.[1] But the main purpose of these incidents,
as of the form of the travel-story which the writer takes over
from the older tradition, is to produce a Gospel which could be
used for the instruction of converts and the edification of the
faithful no less than the earlier accounts of the life of Jesus. Such
a book must be firmly anchored in the historical tradition. We
may regret that the writer used for the purpose the most startling
miracles he could find and that he frankly uses the miracles as
proofs of the glory of Jesus; but in this he is simply following
the tradition of the second Christian generation.

As against these episodes we have others, which may or may
not be drawn from the older historical tradition, but which serve
frankly as illustrations of the main theme, the exposition of Jesus
as the Logos.[2] This is accomplished in the form of a discourse

[1] For the miracle of Cana cf. Achilles Tatius, Leuc. et Clit. 2. 2 (Dionysus
at Tyre) and Pausanias 6. 26. 1 (cult of Dionysus at Elis and Andros.) The
story replaces the synoptic logion on new wine and old bottles; it is perhaps
intended to contradict the saying preserved in Lk. 5. 39 in which Jesus says
that it is impossible for the Pharisees to realize that their whole outlook is
wrong (cf. Creed, ad loc.; the saying is clearly authentic in view of its
contrast with the general outlook of the Gospels, though not in its original
context. The saying may well have been used in support of Judaism or
a judaizing Christianity.) The story of Cana can hardly have been invented
by the evangelist, who belongs to a type of Christianity which is keenly
aware of the distinction between Christianity and paganism; it would seem
to be due to the fancy of popular Christianity in Galilee or Syria, but the
doctrinal implications are no doubt due to the evangelist.

[2] The incidents may have a symbolical value of their own, as well as a
thaumaturgic value where they are miracles, as in the raising of Lazarus;
they may be merely occasions for a discourse, as in the case of Nicodemus
and the woman of Samaria. They may have some historical foundation, but
it is entirely irrelevant. Some of the incidents of the former class appear
to be derived from incidents in the synoptic Gospels (possibly transmitted
by a different line of tradition). Thus the paralytic of 5. 1 ff. seems to be
identical with Mk. 2. 1 ff.; the warning 'sin no more' replaces the forgive-
ness of Mk. 2. 5, since the Church by now is quite confident of her own power
to forgive sins and the old controversy has been forgotten; the word κράβαττος
is almost decisive, since the term in the N.T. is confined to these two incidents
and the very Palestinian source from which Luke drew Acts 5. 15 and 9. 33.
(For the word itself cf. Voc. Gr. N.T., s. voc.) It is typical of Luke's carelessness in revision that he leaves the word here but omits it in his Gospel
(5. 17 ff.) Hence it is also probable that the man born blind is simply the
blind man of Mk. 8. 22 ff. (note the contact between Mk. 8. 23 and Jno. 9. 6),
the fact that he was born blind being added merely for the thaumaturgic value.
Similarly the apparently inartistic anticipation of the anointing at Bethany in

by Jesus, fitted into a dialogue in which the hearers are allowed to interject an occasional question which serves to show their own stupidity or malice in failing to understand what they have heard. In some cases the discourses are preceded by a miracle with a thaumaturgic value of its own; elsewhere the historical element is a mere setting similar to that which we find in the hermetic writings and in the Platonic dialogues. As in the hermetic writings, the questions are usually answered with a rebuke which they do not deserve, for the utterances are normally so cryptic as to be unintelligible to anyone who heard them for the first time. But they are intelligible to the initiated Christian reader, who is thus able to congratulate himself on his superiority to the character in the story.[1] It must be added that in some of these discourse-dialogues we have not merely the intention of expounding the revelation of God in Jesus as the Logos, but the further purpose of answering Jewish objections to Christianity as put forward in the wranglings of Church and synagogue in the hellenistic world.

(1) Nicodemus is introduced in order to offer an opening for a discourse on regeneration and so on baptism. 'Regeneration' was entirely alien to Judaism. It seems to have been penetrating the world of hellenistic theology in the first century, perhaps as a result of its vogue in some of the mystery-cults; in Christian

the story of Lazarus in 11. 2 (for its difficulty cf. Bauer, ad loc.) is probably due to the fact that the evangelist is rewriting the story of the widow's son at Nain and has in mind the Lucan story of the anointing; it is possible that the two stories reached him in a form in which they were not separated by a block of Q material; it is worth noting that the story in Lk. 7. 37 f. is almost as bad Greek as that of the widow's son (cf. above, Lecture I, p. 1).

The change of scene from Galilee to Jerusalem in some of these incidents means nothing. The evangelist is writing for a Church (at Ephesus?) which is too far from Palestine to be interested in Galilee. He cannot entirely eliminate Galilee from his tradition, but he could and did transfer the bulk of the action to a less remote region which had a greater symbolical value.

[1] Scott, 1. 47, points out that few if any of the hermetic writings can be dated in their present form to an earlier date than A.D. 150, but that each tract must be judged on its merits. 'Hermetic' literature may have been known in Jerusalem before the destruction of the Temple (*Gentiles*, 113); cf. also Dodd, *The Bible and the Greeks*, 201 ff. for the date of the Poimandres. For the antiquity of the dialogue-revelation form cf. Reitzenstein, *Poimandres*, 131 ff. It seems probable that the evangelist's dialogues are based on an adaptation of this convention to the synoptic tradition in which reminiscences of actual conversations between Jesus and His disciples or strangers were preserved.

theology it simply replaces the death and resurrection symbolism in which St. Paul had expressed the new life received by the Christian as a result of his conversion and baptism.[1] Nicodemus' stupidity opens the way for a denunciation of Judaism. If it rejects the 'earthly things' of the ordinary synoptic tradition, how can it hope to understand 'heavenly things', the truth that the divine Logos, who has freedom to move as He wills between earth and heaven, is now manifested in the Messianic Son of Man, whose coming exaltation on the Cross is a symbol of His exaltation to heaven?[2] Here the normal Hellenistic conception of a divine element of mind or reason, acting as the intermediary between earth and heaven, is joined to an allegorical interpretation of Moses' serpent[3] which is purely Christian; Judaism found

[1] See Note I on Regeneration. The passage is a rewriting of the Pauline theology of Ro. 6. 3 ff. in terms of the new birth instead of death and resurrection; the arbitrary action of the Spirit, which blows where it wills and produces the new birth in one and not another is another way of expressing the doctrine of predestination of Ro. 9. 9 ff. For the play on the double meaning of πνεῦμα cf. Philo, De Plant. 24, where we have the same contrast of 'up' and 'down', it being the function of the divine 'spirit' to raise man's mind (especially that of the true philosopher) 'up' to heaven, as Moses was called 'up' to God in Lev. 1. 1. For the double meaning of ἄνωθεν as either 'a second time' or 'from heaven' cf. Hoskyns and Davey, ad loc.

Note that in Philo, Q. in Exod. 2. 46 (see Note I) we have a call upwards (*sursum*, i.e. to the top of Mount Sinai symbolical of heaven), equated to the 'new birth' of the prophet.

[2] Verses 8 and 12 ff. imply the conceptions of Eph. 4. 9 ff., for which see *Gentiles*, 195. Properly the element of 'spirit' is in a state of continual passing from earth to heaven and back, and it is this continual interchange that preserves the cosmos in being. In man this element of 'spirit' takes the form of 'mind' (Posidonius ap. Diog. Laert. 7. 139, cf. Philo, De Mund. Op. 69 where man's mind is the image of God, and 135 where the soul is a divine 'spirit' bestowed on him to make him immortal). Thus the element of mind in man can move freely between earth and heaven (cf. Ps.-Arist. De Mund. 1. 2 where mind enables the soul to roam at will θείῳ ψυχῆς ὄμματι τὰ θεῖα καταλαβοῦσα. Cf. also Corp. Herm. 4. 5, 10. 24 b; Seneca, Ep. 14. 4 (92). 30). In Corp. Herm. 16. 5 the sun is the creator who unites οὐσία from above with matter below; but, if there be such a thing as intelligible substance, the mass of the sun is composed of it and his light is the receptacle of it (Scott emends on the ground that it is nonsense to describe the ὄγκος of the sun as composed of νοητὴ οὐσία, but I am not clear that the hermetic writers are incapable of nonsense of this kind). The capacity of 'mind' to move between earth and heaven and to enable man to do the same is simply transferred to Jesus. The 'son of Man' is needed here to emphasize the concrete reality of the Christian redeemer in view of the fact that He has just been described in terms of 'mind'.

[3] For the puzzle cf. Philo, Leg. Alleg. 2. 81, De Agric. 95 f. The typology

it hard to see how a serpent could be the means of salvation; Christianity found it easy, since the serpent was lifted up upon the pole which was the type of the Cross. The writer appends a homily in which 'judgment' as an act of God is abandoned in favour of the view that those who reject the offer of salvation condemn themselves. Thus the evangelist avoids the difficulty of the association of Christianity with the 'wrath of God', just as Philo does[1]; the phrase was too firmly fixed in his tradition to be eliminated entirely, but it is relegated to 3. 36, where it is made clear that it is simply a way of describing the state of those who deliberately reject the light and life that God offers in His Son; the testimony of the Baptist here gives an interesting specimen of the writer's relation to the older tradition; he represents the Baptist as giving the correct interpretation of the synoptic Logion (Mk. 2. 19) as to the children of the bride-chamber, while the 'bride' who appears here is the Church of Eph. 5. 23.[2] At the end of John's testimony the author sums up his conception of Jesus as the heavenly being who comes down to bestow the gifts which the earthly cannot receive.[3] This explains the rejection of Jesus and the Gospel by the majority of mankind. Those who receive Him testify their acceptance of the full truth of God which He utters; for there is no measure which limits God's gift of the spirit to Jesus or to the same gift as handed on by Jesus to the disciple, apparently a criticism of the phrase 'the measure of the gift of Christ' in Eph. 4. 7.[4]

here makes the exaltation of the serpent a type of the 'exaltation' of Jesus on the Cross, this being itself a type of His exaltation to heaven and His power to confer eternal life on the believer. It is perhaps worth noting that in Hipp. El. 5. 16. 6 f. we have apparently a purely Jewish Peratic system, in which Moses' serpent is the true and perfect serpent, the 'power' which accompanied Moses. (The duplicate account in 10 f. is a Christian version.) It is therefore possible that the serpent of Moses was in some Jewish exegesis a type of a 'power' or the Logos. The Fourth Gospel in any case substitutes the Cross as the exaltation of Jesus for the Pauline 'scandal' of so accursed a death by introducing a *testimonium* in which such an exaltation 'on a tree' had already been a means of salvation.

[1] Q.D.S.I. 51; it need hardly be said that Philo none the less leaves 'the wrath of God' to stand as he finds it in his sources quite frequently, e.g. De Somn. 2. 179, De Vit. Moys. 1. 6.

[2] The conception might of course be drawn from the general Christian tradition, but the echoes of Eph. in this part of the Gospel suggest that we have the same source here.

[3] For 'coming from heaven' cf. the position of mind in Philo, Q.D.P.I.S. 84 f., Q.R.D.H. 184 and 274.

[4] The obscurity of the passage has led to the insertion of ὁ θεός as subject

(2) The discourse at the well of Samaria reverses Philo's procedure. Philo had before him the two figures of Wisdom and the
Logos as more or less personal intermediaries between God and
the cosmos. Neither had any real meaning for Judaism, except in
so far as they served to make it intellectually respectable, and
Philo simply identifies the two. But the development of the
Christian doctrine of the Holy Spirit needed two such figures,
and so the evangelist takes over the standing equation of Wisdom
with the waters of the O.T., and identifies Wisdom not with the
Torah but with the Holy Spirit.[1] This is offered by Jesus to all
who, like the woman, are in the natural or psychic condition, a
condition represented by her six husbands, for six is the number
of the material world and the natural soul is not and cannot be
her true husband[2]; while she is in this state she can only think

of διΔωσιν in v. 34. Hoskyns and Davey, ad loc., rightly point out that the
obscurity is due to the double character of Jesus as both recipient and giver
of the Spirit. It seems that the writer is concerned to remove any suspicion
that there is some measure in the giving of the Spirit, as might be suggested
by Eph. 4. 7, and that the obscurity is really due to his assumption that
the reader would understand the allusion. It may be noted that in 7. 39 the
limitation of the Spirit to the period after the glorification of Jesus reflects
Eph. 4. 8 ff.

[1] Cf. Gentiles, 87 ff., for the equation of Wisdom with water. There is a
specially instructive instance in De Fug. et Inv. 195 ff., where Rebecca's well
= divine Wisdom = the source of the particular sciences. But as called
Kadesh = holy it proves that the Wisdom of God has no earthly admixture.
All this is from Philo's secular source. Philo adds either from another source,
or from his own imagination, an entirely new and more edifying exegesis
on the supreme 'source of life' and the drink of immortality. But he has
quite forgotten his symbolism and makes God, not His Wisdom, this supreme
'fountain'. For the identity of Wisdom and the Logos in Philo cf. Gentiles,
loc. cit.

[2] The five husbands are the five senses and the sixth man the natural soul
which can never be the true 'husband' of the highest element in man, which
can only be the Spirit. Heracleon, ap. Orig. in Jo. 13. 11, is right in his
interpretation. But Heracleon is working in terms of a developed Christianity
in which the ogdoad has replaced the hebdomad as the perfect number.
Thus the woman's true husband in the Pleroma has to be her eighth and
not her seventh husband; consequently Heracleon altered the text to make
six husbands and a seventh 'man'; it is not clear how Heracleon explained
him as against her πλήρωμα, who is her 'eighth'.

For six as the number of the created world cf. Philo, Leg. Alleg. 1. 4 and 16,
Q.D.S.I. 12, where six is the number of those who are only capable of the
second best. Since the number is given by the days of creation and the world
was created very good, Philo normally forgets that matter is evil when he
deals with the number six; hence six is normally a fairly good number, but
cf. De Spec. Legg. 2. 58. For the number six as thoroughly evil cf. Ir. Haer.

of worship in terms of Jerusalem and Gerizim. It may be that the woman's departure to tell her friends is borrowed from the hermetic convention,[1] but it may only be an instance of the writer's gift for telling a vivid story;[2] in any case it leaves the stage clear for a conversation between Jesus and His disciples which reveals Him as being like Moses on Sinai above all need of earthly food. This is a favourite theme in Philo; it enables the evangelist to include by implication the fast of Jesus in the wilderness; the synoptic story of the Temptation could hardly be accommodated to his Christology, and the angels were to be avoided where possible in writing for Gentile readers.[3] The result of the meeting of Jesus with the Samaritans is his recognition as the 'saviour of the world', a suitable title in such half-heathen circles.[4]

The next chapter (c. 5) only concerns us here as showing the freedom with which the author treats his sources; Jesus goes to Galilee because He is not honoured in His own country, Judaea. On the other hand, the healing of the paralytic is transferred from Galilee to Jerusalem; it is made the occasion for a long wrangle between Jesus and the Jews, i.e. between the Church and the synagogue at Ephesus, on the position of Jesus as having power

5. 28. 2, 29. 2, and 30, and Rev. 13. 18. (Charles, ad loc., asks 'why 666 and not simply 6 or 66?' obviously the triple repetition intensifies the malignity of the number.)

[1] Cf. Corp. Herm. 1. 27 f.

[2] Note his use of the Marcan trick of dovetailing two stories into one, cf. Rawlinson on Mk. 3. 22 ff.; it is, of course, possible that the story here has some historical basis, but the vivid details are drawn from the story-teller's art, cf. Windisch in Εὐχαριστήριον (*Forsch. z. Rel. u. Lit. d. a. u. n. T.* 19. 2. 211).

[3] Cf. Philo, De Vit. Moys. 2 (3). 69, De Mut. Nom. 258, De Somn. 1. 36. The first and last passages refer to Moses' fast in the wilderness, Exod. 34. 28. For heavenly food in general cf. below, p. 66. It is characteristic of the difference between the Fourth Gospel and Philo that the doing of the will of God replaces contemplation as the food of the soul. For the Fourth Gospel's avoidance of angels cf. above, p. 59, n. 1 and De Gig. 16. In many places Philo introduces angels from the O.T. tradition with no hesitation; here we learn that souls, demons, and angels are the same, except that some of the highest class of souls never enter into bodies; it seems that demons are simply the souls of the wicked. By taking this view ἄχθος βαρύτατον ἀποθήσῃ Δεισιδαιμονίαν; the similarity of the language to Plut. De Is. et Os. 11. 355d suggests a common philosophic commonplace as the source. Cf. Plut. De Superst. 1 (164e) and 14 (171e).

The verses which follow seem to represent an adaptation of Mt. 9. 37 (=Lk. 10. 2) to the second Christian generation; the 'others' are really the Apostles of the first generation.

[4] Cf. above, p. 42.

K

on earth to forgive sins and as lord of the sabbath stated in terms of the author's theology. It concludes with an incidental recognition of the eschatological tradition of the Church, which is thus tactfully relegated to the background, and culminates in a general appeal to the miracles of Jesus and the testimonies of the O.T.[1]

(3) The feeding of the 5,000 and the walking on the water seem to have acquired a fixed place in the Gospel tradition from a very early date; the former incident has already acquired a eucharistic significance in one form of the Marcan tradition.[2] The Fourth Gospel uses it in order to expound its eucharistic theology and at the same time to comply with the hellenistic tradition that the actual words of the mysteries should not be made public.[3] The miracle leads to a discourse, beginning with a cryptic allusion to meat which does not perish. A stupid question enables Jesus to reveal Himself as the true 'Bread from Heaven',[4] i.e. the Logos of which the manna was a standing type,[5] just as water was a standing type of the divine Wisdom.

[1] For vv. 39 and 46 cf. Lk. 24. 27 and 44, and for 41 f. Mk. 12. 38: for the interpretation of the passage cf. Holtzmann, *Joh.-Ev.* 101.

[2] For the eucharistic significance of Mk. 8. 1 ff., cf. above p. 4. The Johannine story opens with a 'departure' which should be from Jerusalem, where Jesus was left in 5. 47, but v. 24 implies Capernaum. The miracle of walking on the water separates the feeding from the discourse on the Bread of Life, and the hiatus has to be mended by the not very satisfactory insertion of 22–4. It would seem that the two incidents had acquired a standing claim to be part of any 'Gospel' and that the evangelist inserted them as a whole from his source. (For 22–4 cf. Hoskyns and Davey, ad loc.)

[3] For this view of 'mysteries' as applied to Judaism by Philo cf. *Gentiles*, 30. It is at any rate the case that while the earliest narrative in the N.T. I Cor. 11. 23 describes the Last Supper in a way that makes it clear that the eucharist is a commemoration of that incident and implies quite clearly the repetition of the words of institution, the Marcan narrative implies nothing of the kind except to the initiated reader, while the Fourth Gospel has dissociated the eucharist from the Last Supper completely. Cf. also *Jerusalem*, 380.

[4] The request for a sign comes from the Marcan sequel to the second miracle of feeding, in which there was no walking on the water, Mk. 8. 11. It would seem that if the Fourth Gospel is not actually following Mk. or Mt. the writer has before him a source in which both forms of the incident appeared. The request is used in order to make the Jews allude to Moses and so lead up to the theme of the 'bread from heaven', just as the woman's allusion to Jacob's well leads up to the living water in 4. 12. The earlier part of the dialogue between Jesus and the Jews enables the evangelist to introduce the Pauline doctrine of faith and works (6. 28 f.).

[5] Cf. Philo, Leg. Alleg. 2. 86, 3. 172 ff.; Q.D.P.I.S. 118; Q.R.D.H. 79, 191. In Leg. Alleg. 3. 173 and De Fug. et Inv. 137 manna is a logos or ῥῆμα for

Jesus is this true bread of life, and faith in Him is the means of securing the salvation which He has been sent to bring to earth. The objection of the Jews that He is merely the son of Joseph leads to a fresh wrangle between the Church and the synagogue, dealing with the theme of Jesus as the revelation in the flesh of the divine life of the world, symbolized by the bread from heaven. This leads to the objection 'How can this man give us His flesh to eat?' The answer is an insistence on the necessity of eating the flesh and drinking the blood of Jesus, which even the disciples find it hard to understand. The purpose of this section of the discourse (vv. 52 ff.) is to proceed from the theology of Jesus as the Logos of whom the manna was a type to the evangelist's eucharistic theology. He insists strongly on the necessity of the actual eating and drinking; but he insists no less firmly on the typically hellenistic explanation of the rite in terms of the words of Jesus which are 'spirit' and 'life'.[1] The difficulty felt by the disciples is intended to impress the Church with the need of understanding the 'spiritual' meaning of the eucharist; hence it is only raised after they have left the synagogue at Capernaum, which has not been favoured with the spiritual explanation and so typifies the present cavils of the Jews at the Christian rite.[2]

the simple reason that in Exod. 16. 15 ff. (LXX), manna is the ῥῆμα 'which the Lord has commanded you to eat'.

[1] For this 'hellenization' of the Gospel cf. Plut. De Is. et Os. 2. 351 *e*, 3. 352*c*, cf. 11. 355*c*, where to observe the rite and understand it in a philosophical manner is the surest guard against both superstition and atheism (cf. p. 65, n. 2 for this passage). Cf. also Dio Chrys. Or. 3. 52 and 31. 15 and especially 4. 41 where the Homeric Διοτρεφεῖς is explained ἢ ἄλλο τι οἴει λέγειν αὐτὸν τὴν τροφὴν ταύτην ἢ Διδασκαλίαν καὶ μαθητείαν. For a similar use of the metaphor of eating and drinking cf. Corp. Herm. 1. 29 (for this passage cf. Kroll, *Lehre d. Herm. Trism.* 373, n. 1). It is possible that this passage refers to a cult in which drinking played a part. But any myth or rite in which eating or drinking appeared had to be explained as a symbol of 'assimilating' knowledge, virtue, &c., and from this the language could be extended to the 'assimilation' of such qualities in rites in which there was no eating or drinking at all, e.g. Philo, Q.D.P.I.S. 85, where the conventional Stoic argument that man's upright position proves his heavenly origin is explained as meaning that he is intended to live on Olympian and incorruptible food. Philo is not here expounding any O.T. story of eating and drinking, and the word 'Olympian' suggests a pagan source. In the same way we meet with λογικαὶ θυσίαι in passages which are not concerned with sacrifice as such, e.g. Ro. 12. 1, Corp. Herm. 13. 19; Philo, Q.D.P.I.S. 21 from a source condemning all sacrifice, where true worship is that of the soul which brings truth as its only sacrifice. For v. 63 cf. Ps.-Arist. De Mund. 4. 9.

[2] We have no account of early controversies between Jews and Christians as to the eucharist, unless they lie behind the charge of 'Thyestean banquets'

It need hardly be said that the reading of this 'spiritual' meaning into a received piece of traditional cultus is entirely hellenistic.[1]

(4) The chapters which follow (7–9) are entirely concerned with the controversy between Church and synagogue, thrown back into the life of Jesus. For the most part they do not concern us: but some points are of interest as showing the hellenistic influence at work, such as the challenge of Jesus' brethren that He must go to Jerusalem for the feast of Tabernacles, not because it is his duty as a pious Jew, but in order that He may make an ἐπίδειξις at Jerusalem as a Greek sage or sophist might do at Olympia.[2] It is possible that the insistence on circumcision as implied in Judaism is due to the fact that it was the weak point in Jewish missionary propaganda. It may well be that it was St. Paul and the Church rather than the Jews who insisted on making it the test question in regard to Gentile observance of the Torah.[3] Jesus uses the occasion of the Feast of Tabernacles with its ceremonies of water-drawing and its illuminations to proclaim the offer of the living water of the Spirit to those who believe in Him and to proclaim Himself as the light of the world, a typical formula of the hellenistic age for the self-revelation of a divine being. For the rest the chapters are a long wrangle with the Jews[4] except that 8. 31, the quite unprovoked

which the Jews are accused of originating by Justin (Dial. 17. 235 a, 108. 335 c), though Trypho rejects it (10. 227 b); cf. Orig. c. Cels, 6. 27, perhaps only repeating Justin. Thus it is possible that the Jews are only introduced in order to lead up to the 'spiritual' interpretation; Christians who reject it are no better than Jews.

[1] The end of the chapter (66–9) seems to be the Johannine version of the confession at Caesarea Philippi. As yet St. Peter only recognizes Jesus as 'the Holy One of God', a term reserved in the synoptic tradition for the devils (Mk. 1. 24, Lk. 4. 34), and one of the disciples who join in the confession 'is a devil'. On the other hand vv. 64 and 70 f., forecasting the betrayal of Judas, reveal to the Christian reader the connexion between the evangelist's eucharistic theology and the synoptic story of the Last Supper.

[2] Cf. above, p. 13, n. 1, Lucian's account of Peregrinus and Dio Chrys. Or. 8. 6 ff. for the Greek practice. Str.-B., ad loc., quote no parallels from Judaism for great teachers using the festivals at Jerusalem to display their ability.

[3] For the necessity of circumcision as a weakness of Jewish missionary propaganda cf. Nock, St. Paul, 104; Gentiles, 62; for the readiness of the less strict Jewish missionary to avoid the issue cf. Jos. Antt. 20. 40.

[4] The whole of these two chapters are an interesting specimen of the author's methods. The attitude of Jesus' brethren is taken from Mk. 3. 21, but at v. 6 they become representatives of Jewish Christians whose 'time is always ready' in the sense that they refuse to be persecuted with the

attack of Jesus on the Jews who believe in Him, is really an attack on claims to superiority made by Jewish Christians; but at v. 39 [1] this point is allowed to lapse out of sight and we return to a general attack on the Jews [2] culminating in the words 'before

Cross of Christ. In 7. 14 ff. the quite unmotived charge that the Jews seek to kill Jesus goes back to Mk. 3. 4 ff., interpreted as meaning that the Jews who condemn Jesus for doing good on the sabbath are themselves breaking it by plotting on it to kill Him; it is possible that this is the correct interpretation of Mk. 3. 4. At 32 ff. we have a fresh controversy; the Jews maintain that Jesus is not the Messiah since the Jews have rejected Him and the Church has only succeeded in converting the Gentiles (cf. Ro. 9. 1 ff.). Jesus' words, of course, cover His Ascension and the subsequent conversion of the Gentiles, and thus form a prophecy which guarantees the truth of His claims (cf. Justin, Dial. 35. 253 *b*). At v. 40 we have a new objection; Jesus cannot be the Messiah, since He was not born at Bethlehem (at v. 27 the argument is that he cannot be the Messiah since the Messiah's birth-place is unknown; for this cf. Gunkel, *Schöpf. u. Chaos*, 198 ff.). The return of the officers is probably motived by the desire to finish the story begun at v. 32, but it enables the evangelist to deal with the objection that no educated Jews have been converted (Orig. c. Cels. 1. 27 and 62). In 8. 12 ff., we have a singularly infelicitous attempt to meet the Jewish objection to the whole position accorded to Jesus by the Church, followed by a repetition of the argument of 7. 34 as to the rejection of the Jews in favour of the Gentiles as a result of the 'exaltation' of Jesus.

[1] The attack on the believing Jews is entirely unwarranted by the story; it is based on a line of argument drawn from Gal. and Ro. Knowledge of the truth (= here the Pauline faith) is the only means of deliverance from the bondage to sin which rests on Jews no less than on Gentiles (Ro. 3. 9 ff., 6. 16 ff.); the Jew can claim no special prerogative as the seed of Abraham (Gal. 3. 16). Only the Son can abide in the house for ever, not the slave (Gal. 4. 3 ff.); the fact that the slave is really not the slave of God to whom the house belongs but of sin is overlooked. True freedom only comes through the Son by some unspecified method of liberation which replaces the Pauline 'adoption as sons'. The evangelist treats the theme so freely that it is impossible to say whether he has the Pauline writings in mind or is following the common tradition of the Church. Whether a specifically Jewish Christianity survived as an organized force when the Gospel was written is perhaps doubtful; it is quite possible that the argument is simply a specimen of an apologetic convention surviving after it has lost its real relevance.

[2] At 39 ff. we pass to arguments which are quite inappropriate as against Jews who believe on Jesus, whether in His lifetime at Jerusalem or as Jewish Christians. It is possible that v. 41 refers to Jewish scandals as to the birth of Jesus (Orig. c. Cels. 1. 28; for the Jewish version cf. Klausner, *Jesus of Nazareth*, 23 f.). But there is no trace of any scandal to the effect that Jesus was of Samaritan origin (v. 48), which makes it possible that in v. 41 the Jews are replying to arguments of the Church modelled on Gal. 4. 22. As against this must be set the fact that the charge that Jesus has a devil in v. 48 is a perfectly genuine one (Mk. 3. 21 ff.); hence it seems likely that the

Abraham was, I am'. We have here the most striking instance of the evangelist's fondness for a solemn pronouncement in this form, which represents a conflation of the words in which Jahveh proclaims Himself to Moses at the Bush with the regular words 'I am' followed by a predicate such as 'the light of the world' in the epiphanies of Gentile religion.[1] The language of Exod. 3. 14 was peculiarly beloved in Jewish exponents of the Torah to the Greeks, since it proved that the God of Israel was really the God of philosophy; He was pure 'being', and even mercy and justice were only attributes of His essential nature.[2]

charge that He is a Samaritan is genuine also. We know too little of the early controversies of Church and synagogue to press the argument from silence.

[1] For the ἐγώ εἰμι formula cf. Reitzenstein, *Poimandres*, 245 f., who is more cautious than such writers as Dibelius, *From Tradition to Gospel* and Bertram, *Leidensgeschichte Jesu*, 53 and 58, in recognizing that the phrase does not always imply an epiphany. For the formula in Gentile religion cf. the aretology of Isis at Andros (for this literature cf. Nock, *Conversion*, 40, and *Gentiles*, 56 ff.), Plutarch, De Is. et Os. 9. 354 c and in *oratio obliqua* Corp. Herm. Exc. 23. 65 ff. In Pap. Mag. Gr. 5. 110 ff. we have a series of the 'I am' form changing to the third person at 135 (for this passage cf. Reitzenstein, *Poimandres*, 184 f.; Dieterich, *Abraxas*, 68). Cf. also the repeated οὗτος of Acts 7. 35 ff. For 'I am the light of the world' cf. Lucian, Alexander 18, and Weinreich, 'Alexander der Lügenprophet', in *Neue Jahrb. f. d. klass. Alt.* 47 (1921) 145 ff. and for ἐγώ εἰμι in general cf. further Norden, *Agnostos Theos*, 186 ff. Cf. also below, p. 73, n. 3, p. 78, n. 3, and p. 87, n. 2.

[2] For the thought of God as pure being in Platonism cf. Festugière, *L'Idéal Rel. chez les Grecs*, 43 ff., and for the impossibility of such an idea in rabbinical Judaism *Judaism*, 1. 361. For Exod. 3. 14 as proving that God is pure being cf. Philo, De Mut. Nom. 11 ff., where the text proves that God is ineffable except as pure being, while the Logos is shown to be equally ineffable by the fact that the angel of Gen. 32. 29 refuses to reveal His name; Gen. 17. 1 shows that God can only be seen under His two powers of justice and goodness, implied in the titles κύριος and θεός. The passage is remarkable as an attempt to combine the Logos with the 'powers' which are properly simply duplicates of the Logos borrowed from a different tradition of Stoic terminology (cf. *Gentiles*, 50 ff.: see also Aristides, Or. 37 (2). 28 (Keil, 2. 312) for Athene as the δύναμις of Zeus: cf. Note on Lecture II, p. 49, n. 1. For God as pure being cf. also Q.D.P.I.S. 160, De Post. Cain. 167, and the use of ὁ ὤν and τὸ ὄν *passim* as a description of God. For an emphatic statement of the pre-existence of the Logos cf. De Sacr. Ab. et Cain. 66. It does not appear that Philo ever actually describes the being who appears to Moses in the burning bush as the Logos; the incident was too much the foundation of Judaism for him to do so. But it is implied in De Somn. 1. 231 ff. that it was not the supreme Being but an angel; immediately before this the 'god' who appears in Gen. 31. 13 was the Logos, while in 239 he is 'the image of God τὸν ἄγγελον αὐτοῦ λόγον'. For similar views outside Judaism cf. Kroll, *Lehre d. Herm. Trism.* 2 ff., but it is doubtful whether the bare 'I am' would have been used at this period by any but a Jewish writer;

Thus Jesus here practically proclaims Himself as the Logos of the God of pure being, who appeared to Moses at the bush; it is scarcely surprising that the Jews should seek to stone Him. The last of the three chapters is one of the evangelist's most brilliant pieces of story-telling; its object is to connect the healings of the blind in the synoptic tradition with Jesus as the light of the world, rejected by the Pharisees to their condemnation, but accepted by the Gentiles who receive the apostolic message.[1]

(5) The next section, dealing with Jesus as the door of the sheep, is so abrupt in its opening as to suggest that it was once an independent tract or homily, perhaps more than one. Jesus as 'the Door' may be drawn from the synoptic Gospels (Mt. 7. 13; Lk. 13. 24),[2] but the door leads not to the narrow way but to the fold of the Church. The fold itself however is replaced by the shepherd. The Good Shepherd has obvious connexions with the O.T.; apart from Ps. 23. 1 we find that both God and the rulers of Israel are shepherds. As regards rulers it must be remembered that according to hellenistic ideas a king might be regarded as divine, or as the possessor of a soul drawn from a higher region of the cosmos than the ordinary run of mankind.[3] Thus the king could be in an intermediate state between God and man; the thought could be adapted to Judaism if it was given a suitable moralizing turn.[4] Again, since the shepherd is of a higher order of being than the sheep, it follows that the king is aptly symbolized by the shepherd,

the absence of a predicate is made possible by Exod. 3. 14 and the traditional Jewish interpretation of the name of Jahveh.

[1] He washes in the pool which is ἀπεσταλμένος. I owe the point to Professor C. H. Dodd.

[2] The door as a symbol does not appear in Philo, and it is possible that the symbolism is based on the language of the synoptic tradition; but it is, of course, possible that it was once popular in hellenistic Judaism. The whole passage is confused; we begin with the Apostle who comes in through the door and is admitted by the door-keeper (? Jesus) and takes his sheep out of the fold of Judaism; but by this time the shepherd is not the Apostle but Jesus (v. 4 b). We then have the two 'parables' of the door and the shepherd.

[3] For this conception going back to the 'hermetic' astrology of the Ptolemaic age cf. Cumont, L'Ég. des Astr. 26.

[4] Corp. Herm. Exc. 24. 1 ff. (Scott, 494); especially compare 3 with Philo, fr. ex Ant. Mel. ser. 104 (M. 2. 673) τῇ μὲν οὐσίᾳ ἴσος τοῦ παντὸς ἀνθρώπου ὁ βασιλεύς, τῇ ἐξουσίᾳ δὲ τοῦ ἀξιώματος ὅμοιός ἐστι τῷ ἐπὶ πάντων θεῷ· οὐκ ἔχει γὰρ ἐπὶ γῆς ἑαυτοῦ ὑψηλότερον· χρὴ τοίνυν καὶ ὡς θνητὸν μὴ ἐπαίρεσθαι καὶ ὡς θεὸν μὴ ὀργίζεσθαι· εἰ γὰρ καὶ εἰκόνι θεϊκῇ τετίμηται, ἀλλὰ καὶ κόνει χοϊκῇ συμπέπλεκται.

since he is of a higher orders of being than his subjects. The classical title 'shepherd of the people' could thus become an argument for the divinity of the Emperor.[1]

But we have also in Philo the view that the task of a shepherd is so noble that God Himself can be so described, as in Ps. 23. 1, where God is said to rule the cosmos through the agency of right Logos, His only begotten son, who is identical with the angel of Exod. 23. 20. God can equally be described as the shepherd of the soul; a soul so shepherded lacks nothing.[2]

Thus we have God as the shepherd of the cosmos ruling it through His Logos; and any divine being could be the shepherd of the cosmos.[3] Thus the Good Shepherd was admirably suited to the evangelist's theme, for it implied the combination in Jesus of the higher nature of the Logos with a human character which preserves to the full the human appeal of the Christ of the synoptic Gospels.[4] The discourse is broken by

[1] Cf. Philo, Leg. ad G. 76 (for Philo's source here cf. above, p. 48), and Dio Chrys. Or. 1. 18; here the commonplace takes the form that if the shepherd cares for sheep which are of a lower order, much more must the king care for men who are of the same order; in Philo, as in the hermetic form, the argument is that as the shepherd is of a higher order than the sheep, so the king is of a higher order than his subjects (the view is that of Caligula).

[2] De Agric. 44 ff., where Moses' prayer (Num. 27. 16 f.) is a prayer that the true ruler, the ὀρθὸς λόγος, may not leave the flock in us untended; 'right reason' in the Microcosm corresponds to the Logos in the cosmos (ib. 51; the same theme recurs De Post. Cain. 68). The presence of the true ruler delivers the soul from ochlocracy, the worst form of government, and establishes the best, democracy; it equally expels 'tyranny', the state when mind rules for its own ends. Thus democracy only exists when the soul is ruled by mind for unselfish ends. We might suppose that Philo was a democrat (cf. De Conf. Ling. 108, De Spec. Leg. 4. 237, De Virt. 180 for the contrast of democracy with ochlocracy). But in De Abr. 242 democracy only comes into being when right reason makes war on the nine kings, the five senses and the four passions. Thus democracy requires right reason as its autocrat; in other words we have a defence of the principate of Augustus as combining the benefits of democracy and monarchy. Cf. Aristides, Or. 26 (14), 38 (Keil, 2. 102) where the imperial system is better than any democracy and ib. 90 (Keil, 2. 118) where it combines the benefits of the three classical forms of government.

[3] Cf. Hipp. El. 5. 8. 34 and 9. 9 where Attis in the Nassene hymn is the 'shepherd of the white stars'. In the epitaph of Abercius the good shepherd has 'eyes which see everywhere'. The eyes of God might be Jewish or Christian but hardly apply to the Good Shepherd except as the eyes of the cosmic Logos, i.e. the sun and moon. For Abercius cf. *Dict. d'Arch. Chrét.* 1. 66 ff.

[4] The theme of God or kings as shepherds though not unknown to the

debates among the Jews and a further controversy between them and Jesus;[1] the theme of the Good Shepherd is resumed at 10. 27 in order to lead up to the saying 'I and my father are one'. The words are irrelevant, if we limit the conception of the Good Shepherd to the O.T. thought of kings and rulers as shepherds. Their purpose is to make it clear that the Good Shepherd is a title of Jesus as the divine Logos. They serve further to justify the Church's belief by using the obvious O.T. crux of Ps. 82. 6 as a testimony; here the evangelist follows the Philonic method of using the more difficult passages of the O.T. as pegs on which to hang his choicest bits of allegory.[2]

rabbis is comparatively rare, cf. Str.-B. on this passage and Lk. 15. 5, where the quotation from Exod. R. 68 *b* looks suspiciously as though it had been modelled on Luke to prove that Moses, not Jesus, is the true 'good shepherd'. Cf. also Ps. Sol. 17. 45 and 1 En. 89. 59 ff. (here the shepherds are probably angels, cf. Charles in *Apocr. and Pseud.*, ad loc.). It is possible that the rabbinical avoidance of the theme is due to its popularity in Christianity; but it is also possible that it was due to the popularity of the theme in paganism; cf. the preceding note, and for the popularity of the 'good shepherd' in pagan art cf. *Dict. d'Arch. Chrét.* 13. 2272 ff. where, however, it is contended that the Hermes Criophoros of Tanagra and similar figures had become purely conventional ornaments before the Christian era as a result of the pastoral tastes of Alexandrine literature. One such pagan figure, Endymion, is perhaps of interest in view of Servius' comment on Verg. Georg. 3. 391, where it is said 'cuius rei mystici volunt quandam secretam esse rationem'. For a Christian 'good shepherd' in an astral setting which suggests a derivation from the pagan motives noted above cf. ib. 1, 3009 ff.

[1] The whole passage is far more coherent if 10. 1–18 be omitted, and the scene at the Feast of Dedication introduces the idea of the sheep quite naturally. It looks as though the evangelist had introduced three pericopae (those who enter by the Door, the Door, and the Good Shepherd) which had an independent existence of their own as homiletic fragments based on the synoptic tradition.

[2] Formally the argument of vv. 34 ff. is that if the scripture calls all the prophets 'gods', much more can Jesus as the chief of God's emissaries and the son of God (for such conceptions of the Logos cf. Philo, De Conf. Ling. 62 and 146) be so described. For the phrase 'I and the Father are one' cf. Corp. Herm. 1. 6 (Scott, 117). Philo can never quite say that God and the Logos are one, for the simple reason that he only introduces the Logos when he wishes to distinguish between God as existing in Himself and God in action towards the cosmos. Hence he could hardly use the language of v. 34, which is simply the evangelist's method of defending the worship offered to Jesus by the Church as compatible with Jewish monotheism. For Philo's use of difficult passages of the O.T. cf. above, Lecture II, p. 35, n. 4; for his use of them as a means of finding an allusion to the Logos in the O.T. cf. De Somn. 1. 228 ff. where the words of Gen. 31. 13 ἐγώ εἰμι ὁ θεὸς ὁ φανείς σοι ἐν τόπῳ θεοῦ do not imply two Gods, since ὁ θεός means God Himself while θεός without the article refers to the Logos. Cf.

The narrative of the raising of Lazarus shows Jesus as the Life of the world, just as the story of the man born blind showed Him as its Light; but in one sense it stands nearer to the synoptic tradition since the miracle depends on the faith of his friends and is not like the miracle of Cana simply a means of producing faith.[1] The debate in the Sanhedrin is remarkable for its insight into Jewish affairs at the period, and is one of the details which suggest that the evangelist was well informed[2]; but the con-

also his predilection for Exod. 7. 1 (De Sacr. Ab. et Cain. 8 ff., Q.D.P.I.S. 161, De Somn. 2. 189, Q.O.P.L. 43; in the first and last Moses is the wise man of Stoic convention). Philo does not refer to Ps. 82. 6, but this is natural in view of the rarity of his reference to the O.T. outside the Pentateuch.

It may be added that the theme of the torch and the flame as used by Philo of the relation between God and His spirit (De Gigant. 25) comes very near to an assertion of the unity of God and the Logos, since the description of the Spirit in 27 shows that it is really identical with the Logos (cf. De Somn. 1. 62). This unity in difference of God and the Logos was essential for any Stoicism which distinguished between the supreme element of deity concentrated in the firmament and the divine element of reason as pervading and ordering the cosmos, i.e. the divine Logos [Bevan, *Stoics and Sceptics*, 43, traces this distinction back to Zeno himself, cf. *Gentiles*, 65].

The nearest parallel to the Johannine language here and at 14. 11 is the σὺ γὰρ εἶ ἐγὼ καὶ ἐγὼ σύ of the magical papyri; for this and for the relation of the Johannine language to hellenistic syncretism cf. below, p. 78.

[1] Miracles were too impressive an argument for the Church to refuse to exploit their thaumaturgic value (Gal. 3. 5; Acts 4. 30, 9. 35, 42, &c.). Unfortunately other cults could produce equally impressive evidence. Hence Justin has to argue in Apol. 1. 30 ff. (72 a) that the prophecies fulfilled in Jesus prove that His miracles are really divine and not due to magic, but in Dial. 7. (225 a) the miracles of the prophets are evidence that they foretold the truth, while the fact that they preached the one true God proves that they were aided by God, not by demons; but ib. 69 f. (296 b) Justin makes the conventional appeal to the miracles of Jesus as evidence of His divinity. Ir. Haer. 2. 48. 2 claims that the miracles of heretics as against those of the Church do no real good to men but only harm; he provides no means for testing this. Orig. c. Cels. 1. 67 defends the miracles of Jesus and the Church as against magic by appealing to the improvement which Christianity produces in the character of the convert. This is the only strong ground; miracles are a poor apologetic argument in a world which believes in magic.

[2] For 'the High Priest of that year' cf. *Jerusalem*, 61 ff., and to the references there given add 2 Macc. 11. 3, showing that the policy of reducing the power of the Oriental priesthoods by making the High Priesthood of the great temples an annual appointment goes back to Seleucid times. We get a glimpse of the gradual process by which a high priesthood for life was turned into an annual office in Strabo's account of the fortunes of his immediate ancestors as priests of Comana in Pontus during and after the Mithridatic wars (Strabo 12. 3. 34 ff., 558). Cf. also T.B. Yôma 8 b.

ception of the High Priest as an *ex-officio* prophet is again that of the Dispersion; Judaism in Palestine knew too much about the high priests to make use of the idealized conception which is taken for granted by Philo.[1] The triumphal entry on Palm Sunday is, of course, a fixed part of the tradition;[2] but to it the evangelist appends the story of the Greeks who came to see Jesus. The 'hour' of the glory of Jesus is not the delusive triumph of the entry into Jerusalem but His death, which is to be followed by the rejection of the Jews and the admission of the Gentiles. The scene ends with a final wrangle, which reflects the claim of the Church to find in Jesus the light of the world, as against the synagogue's futile hope of a triumphant Messiah, followed by a selection of *testimonia* to convict the Jews and a final appeal to them to accept the life and light that is offered to them, put into the mouth of Jesus, but addressed to the Jews of the evangalist's own time and place.

(6) The story of the Last Supper opens with the washing of the disciples' feet.[3] The story in itself is a dramatization of Lk.

[1] For the High Priest as known to the Pharisees cf. Mishnah, Yôma 1. 3 and 5. For the idealized conception of him abroad cf. Philo, De Spec. Leg. 4. 190 ff.; for the High Priest as the bond of unity between the members of the nation ib. 1. 229 ff., and 3. 131. It should be noted that the diffusion of Judaism throughout the world is a common theme (Philo, Leg. ad G. 281 ff., Jos. Antt. 14. 110 ff.). The theme, however, is simply a variation on the theme of the diffusion of the Roman Empire (cf. Leg. ad G. 10 ff.; Dion. Halic. 1. 3; Aristides, Or. 26 (14) 10 ff., 28 ff.; Keil, 2. 94, 100). This theme was obviously suited to panegyrics (for the theme as applied to particular cities cf. Dion. Halic. Ars Rhet. 5. 5); the Jewish variation is quite worthless as evidence that there were really Jews in all the places named. It is possible that the prominence of Annas as against Caiaphas in the Fourth Gospel rests on good tradition; but it is conceivable that the evangelist needed the testimony of Caiaphas to Jesus as an apologetic argument and therefore diverts responsibility from him to Annas in 18. 13, though Caiaphas is too firmly fixed in the tradition to be omitted entirely.

[2] The section 11. 54–7 is at first sight entirely pointless, even if it be supposed to be based on good tradition. The purpose is, however, to get Jesus away from Bethany in order to clear the stage for His triumphal entry, which would hardly be possible if he had been staying in the suburbs. It would seem that the anointing and the triumphal entry were a fixed part of the tradition. The evangelist makes no use of the anointing; the entry is needed (a) for the unconscious testimony of the Pharisees in 12. 19, and (b) for the contrast between the false glory of the entry into Jerusalem and the true glory of the crucifixion and the conversion of the Gentiles, symbolized by the Greeks of 12. 20.

[3] For a selection of interpretations of the scene cf. Hoskyns and Davey, ad loc. The difficulty lies in the fact that the occasion and the symbolism almost compel the reader to see in the foot-washing an allusion to baptism;

22. 27; but its purpose seems to be to contrast the humility of the Lord and of the true disciple (v. 17) with the false disciple, who though baptized (v. 10 f.) and a partaker of the eucharist (v. 18) is none the less a traitor. Jesus' insight then proved His true nature to His disciples (v. 19); the Church, which is confronted with the problem of the traitor and apostate among its members, must not expect to be free from similar perils, but must not be disturbed by them. Here we are within the Christian tradition; but the man who has been washed, but still is not clean because he continues in sin with no intention of repenting, is derived from the theology of the hellenistic world.[1]

but the meaning of the allusion, if it exists, is left obscure. The difficulty is increased by the doubtful reading in v. 10, where the shorter reading makes no sense, unless νίψασθαι be taken as meaning minor ablutions as against complete bathing. But this sense, though possible, is by no means necessary, cf. Philostr. Vit. Apoll. Tyan 8. 7. 7; there are crimes which ἀπονῖψαι οὔτ' ἐμοὶ Δυνατὸν οὔτε τῷ πάντων Δημιουργῷ θεῷ.

[1] The explanation suggested is based on the fact that the scene culminates in the contrast between the rest of the disciples who are clean and Judas who is not in v. 10. This is followed by the homily, based on Lk. 22. 27, which leads up again to the traitor, who is present at the Last Supper as he will be at the eucharist of the Church (v. 19). Possibly v. 20 implies that the traitors are false teachers; those who reject them and receive the true apostles receive Jesus Himself. In any case the emphasis both in the story and in the homily is on the presence of the traitor. This suggests that the evangelist has in mind the theme of the impenitent sinner who takes part in the outward observances of religion; it appears in Philo, Q.D.S.I. 7 ff. (note εὐχαριστικῶς and ἐκνιψάμενοι) and De Spec. Leg. 1. 269, and goes back to Theophrastus, De Pietate (cf. Bernays, *Theophrastos' Schrift über die Frömmigkeit*, 67). The main commonplace of the need of inward as well as outward purity appears in 'Pythagoras', ap. Diod. Sic. 10. 9. 6, but Philo stresses the impenitent sinner; that he is following a pagan source is clear from his reference to 'temples'. (I owe the suggestion that Judas here is the impenitent sinner in the Church to Dr. R. Newton Flew.)

On this explanation we have a contrast between Simon who is clean even though he is shortly to deny Jesus, i.e. the Christian who may fall into sin, and the baptized traitor, i.e. the apostate of the Church. For the problem of the apostate in Judaism cf. Philo, De Virt. 182; cf. also Clem. Alex. Exc. ex Theod. 83 (ed. Casey, 705 ff.), where if the evil spirits go down into the water with a man and gain the seal with him they render him incurable (cf. also below, p. 86, n. 5).

It may be noted that it is proverbial that important tasks should not be undertaken ἀνίπτοις ποσίν (Lucian, Pseudolog. 4 (165), where the deified Ἔλεγχος is reminiscent of Jno. 16. 8 (cf. below, p. 82, nn. 7, 8), Aul. Gell. Noct. Att. 17. 5. 14, Dio Chrys. Or. 12. 43). There is probably no connexion except the same social necessity: the desire of the evangelist to provide a solemn ritual introduction to the supreme revelation of Jesus which is to follow leads to the dramatization of the Lucan logion in a peculiarly impressive form.

(7) The stage is now set for the final revelation, which falls into three parts, each of which might be, and may once have been, a separate tract. Chapter 14 is a complete unit, which is reinforced and expanded in 15 and 16; the High-priestly prayer in 17 is again complete in itself.[1] All three correspond closely to hellenistic models. The first two are in form dialogues with unintelligent interruptions, inserted to underline the vital points (14. 5 Jesus as the way; 14. 9 the unity of Jesus with the Father, 14. 23 love as the condition of receiving revelation, 16. 18 the presence of Jesus through the Spirit in the Church as more important than his bodily presence, 16. 29 the final recognition, which enables the Church to conquer the world). The terminology of the revelation is that of hellenistic theology; Jesus is the hermetic element of Logos or Mind, which as divine is 'in' the Father, as the Father is 'in' Him; on His approaching departure, His place will be taken by the Spirit, who will give them the full knowledge that in the same way the disciple is 'in' Jesus as Jesus is 'in' him. The thought and language are drawn from the doctrine that the man who possesses 'mind' and recognizes its divine nature is thereby delivered from the material and can attain to unity with God, who is Himself mind or the source of that element of mind which orders and rules the cosmos.[2] On the other hand, the content is entirely Christian, for the means of attaining to the revelation is not knowledge of any kind but love,

---

[1] For various views as to the relation of 13 and 14 to 15 and 16 cf. Hoskyns and Davey, 2. 547, and Bauer's detached note at 14. 31. The former reject the idea of any dislocation in the text or change in the author's purpose. This seems quite impossible. From 14. 25–31 we have a solemn peroration ending in one of the abrupt phrases which the author uses to underline his point as in 13. 30 (cf. above, Lect. II, p. 46, n. 1). Here Jesus going from the world to the Father through the Cross calls the disciple to follow; it is entirely inappropriate if followed by three chapters of discourse instead of the road to Gethsemane. It would seem that the evangelist (or a final editor) has simply inserted here another tract on the same theme, which once had an independent existence.

[2] The theme is that of the hermetic Poimandres, which gives the doctrine that the world originates in the fall of a divine being and that man can be saved from it by a divine gift of mind in the form of a revelation. For such revelations cf. Nock, *Conversion*, 107 ff. and notes, p. 289; Reitzenstein, *Poimandres*, 117 ff.; for the use of the form by Philo cf. De Cher. 43 ff., and De Migr. Abr. 8 ff., where we have a solemn proclamation to man to know his true nature as mind and to flee from body and sense and even from all uttered speech in order to attain to his true destiny. For the whole type of missionary speeches put into the form of a revelation of man's nature as a spiritual being and the logical consequences involved cf. Norden, *Agnostos Theos*, 129 ff.

faith, and the keeping of the commandments of Jesus. Thus the end of the revelation is union with God, mediated by Jesus as the divine agent, who provides the Spirit which will enable man to rise from earth to heaven when the mission of the revealer is ended;[1] but the agent is simply the historical Jesus, and the mystery revealed is simply the love of 1 Cor. 13 and the general Christian tradition. Gnosis is replaced by love, for God is love and only 'like can know like'.

Among resemblances of detail we may note that 'the way' appears as a description of the Logos in Philo,[2] while the saying 'I am the way' is one of the 'I am' sayings which we have considered already; the formula 'I am in the Father and the Father in me' goes back to the pantheistic tradition of Stoicism influenced perhaps by the religion of Egypt.[3] It is somewhat

[1] The position of the Spirit is partly dictated by the developing theology of the Church, but it is in keeping with Philo, Leg. Alleg. 1. 38, where the spirit of God enables man to ascend to Him, as Jesus *qua* Logos does in 14. 3 ff., and as the Spirit does by implication in 14. 16 f., where he replaces Jesus as the Paraclete. (For the term cf. Hoskyns and Davey, 2. 549; but the meaning of the word, as in Philo, is simply 'helper', e.g. De Mund. Op. 23 where 'advocate' is out of the question.) For the Spirit as enabling man to rise to heaven cf. also De Plant. 24 and De Vit. Moys. 2 (3). 265 where it ποδηγετεῖ man to the truth (cf. Jno. 16. 13). For the spirit as dwelling in man cf. De Gigant. 19, 28, De Spec. Leg. 4. 49. For the Logos as dwelling in man as Jesus does in 14. 23 cf. De Post. Cain. 122; for God Himself De Somn. 1. 149, 2. 253, but here we simply have the normal Jewish tradition for which the Logos means nothing. Philo could not in the same passage make both the Logos and God dwell in man; in so far as he distinguishes them the Logos would dwell in all but the holiest of men, in whom God would dwell Himself on the principle of De Conf. Ling. 146 and similar passages.

[2] Bauer, ad loc., quotes numerous parallels from the theme of the soul's ascent to heaven. This seems unnecessary, cf. Philo, Q.D.S.I. 142 ff., where Gen. 6. 12 means that all flesh had corrupted wisdom, the straight road which leads to God; wisdom and the Logos are interchangeable. In De Post. Cain. 101 f. the royal road of Num. 20. 17, which figures in Q.D.S.I. loc. cit. reappears as philosophy which 'the Law' calls the ῥῆμα and logos of God (Deut. 28. 14). Cf. also Quaest. in Gen. 4. 125 and Corp. Herm. 4. 11 *b* (Scott, 156), where the εἰκών of God leads man to Him; the εἰκών of God in Philo = the Logos. But it is doubtful whether Jesus would have been represented as describing Himself as 'the way' apart from the synoptic tradition; this is probably the source of the 'living way' of Heb. 10. 20.

[3] For the 'I am' formulae cf. above, p. 70, n. 1, and p. 73, n. 3 for the language here cf. Corp. Herm. 5. 11 and Scott's note on that passage, and the 'Gospel of Eve' *ap.* Epiph. Panar. 26. 3; cf. also Isis' proclamation of herself in Plut. De Is. et Os. 9. 354 *c*. It would seem that here, and in the religious beliefs which lie behind the magical papyri (P.M.G. 8. 38 and 13. 795 ff.), we have Egyptian religion in a Greek dress. But God is 'in'

startling to find that Epictetus in a conventional Stoic-Cynic glorification of Heracles remarks as one proof of his nobility that
he did not leave his children orphans; probably both this and
14. 18 are drawn from a commonplace that no man is an orphan
since God cares for all.[1] The thought of 14. 21 that the revelation
of God is confined to a chosen few selected for their piety is
quite in accordance with the Jewish adaptation of the hellenistic
view that piety and the worship of God go together. Philo interprets this to mean not that gnosis is necessary for piety but
that piety is necessary for attaining to gnosis.[2] The promise of

the Logos in Philo in such passages as De Migr. Abr. 4 ff., De Mund. Op.
20 ff., where the ideal cosmos exists in the Logos just as the plan in the mind
of the architect. Since, however, the ideal cosmos really is the Logos (24),
the architect must be God. Cf. also De Somn. 1. 62, where the Logos is 'the
place' which God fills, while in Leg. Alleg. 1. 44 God is His own 'place'.
It should be observed that here we are dealing with the conception of God
as 'the Place' which at any rate acclimatized itself later in rabbinical
Judaism even if it did not originate there. It would seem that the influence
of Egyptian religion (if any) lies behind the popular philosophy of the Logos
as incorporated by Philo and the general Jewish 'philosophy' of which he
has preserved such ample specimens, and was taken over by the evangelist
in good faith as 'philosophy' suited to express the Christian conception of
the person of Jesus. Thus the Fourth Gospel represents a Judaism derived
from a Stoicism which may have been coloured by Egyptian religion; the
magical papyri reflect Egyptian religion, which had perhaps acquired a
superficial colouring of Greek philosophy.

[1] Epict. Diss. 3. 24. 14. Heracles did not mind leaving behind the children
of his numerous marriages οὐ στένων οὐδὲ ποθῶν οὐδ' ὡς ὀρφανοὺς ἀφιείς since he
believed that no man is an orphan, for he has a father Zeus who cares for him.
If the resemblance here be due to pure coincidence, it is possible to explain
almost any resemblance in the same way; but it is extremely difficult to
suppose that the evangelist was acquainted with Epictetus. But in Philo,
De Spec. Leg. 4. 179 ff., we find that the whole Jewish nation are in a
sense orphans, being cut off from other nations by the Torah and their
superior piety; but they are always assured that God will pity them owing
to the merits of the patriarchs. Philo has in mind Deut. 10. 18; hence the
Jews are not simply 'not orphans' but orphans under divine protection;
cf. ib. 1. 308. The theme in Philo is part of the regular Jewish mission-
propaganda; it probably came to the evangelist from this source, the ultimate
origin of the philosophical commonplace being Plato, Phaedo, 116 a.

[2] Cf. Kroll, Lehre d. Herm. Trism. 353, for the hermetic view (going back
to Posidonius through Cicero and Seneca) that true piety is to know God.
He points out (following Bousset) that in the earlier sources knowledge produces piety, but in the hermetica piety either precedes or accompanies
knowledge, but is unable to account for the change. It is at least possible
in view of the influence of Judaism on the hermetica (cf. Dodd, The Bible
and the Greeks, passim) that the change is due to Jewish influence. For piety
as the necessary condition of the knowledge of God cf. Q.D.S.I. 143 ff. and

a 'manifestation' by Jesus of Himself to His disciples and the thought of God as a guest coming to dwell in man are frequently found in Philo, who also associates the presence of God with peace in the soul, though it is characteristic that while in John it is the presence of God that produces peace, in Philo it is only the soul which attains to internal peace that can hope to become the abode of God.[1]

(8) In c. 15 we have the second version of the same theme. The simile of the true vine appears in the O.T. where Israel figures as a vine, but a vine doomed to destruction (Ps. 80. 9 ff., Is. 5. 1 ff., Jer. 2. 21). Philo, however, interprets the prophecy of Isaiah as meaning that Israel, which is the mind which contemplates God, has for its house the soul, the vineyard of God, which He cultivates in order that it may produce the fruits of virtue.[2] Now Israel in Philo can mean Israel as the nation, God's chosen people,[3] or the contemplative type of mankind, who may be identified by implication with the nation or the best elements in it,[4] or the contemplative soul which is the first-born of God,[5] or the element of mind by which man can see God,[6] or finally the Logos, the divine element in the world which has a special affinity with the highest element in man.[7] Here Jesus the Logos animates the disciples, i.e. the Church, which is the true Israel

De Mut. Nom. 81 where the vision of God (= Israel) is the reward of ascetic virtue (= Jacob). It is possible to attain to gnosis without ἄσκησις, but only if God bestows a free gift of virtue.

[1] For God as ' manifesting' himself cf. De Somn. 1. 228, Leg. Alleg. 3. 101. For God as making His abode in the soul cf. De Cher. 98 ff., De Sobr. 64 (where, when God comes to dwell in man, He raises the little habitation of his mind to heaven, an interesting attempt to harmonize the formally contradictory conceptions, which meet us in 14. 2 ff., and 23 f., and are common in Philo). For peace in v. 27 cf. De Somn. 2. 250 ff., where Jerusalem (= vision of peace) means that those who abandon the sphere of becoming, which is war, attain to peace and so can become the ἐνδιαίτημα καὶ πόλις θεοῦ; it is perhaps worth noting that Philo ascribes his knowledge to a special revelation from τὸ εἰωθὸς ἀφανῶς ἐνομιλεῖν πνεῦμα ἀόρατον: cf. also De Fug. et Inv. 174. The thought seems to be Philo's theologizing of the conception of philosophy in such passages as Epict. Diss. 3. 13. 8 ff.; probably we are dealing with a widespread commonplace.

[2] De Somn. 2. 173.

[3] De Abr. 57, where Israel appear as a new race after the Flood with a special gift of 'seeing God'.

[4] Q.D.S.I. 144; but in 148 it turns out that we are dealing with Israel, cf. De Praem. et Poen. 44; Q.R.D.H. 278 f.

[5] De Post. Cain. 63.   [6] Leg. Alleg. 3. 186.

[7] De. Conf. Ling. 146. For the relation of mind to the Logos cf. De Mund. Op. 139 and 146 (a copy, fragment, or reflection).

in virtue of that union between God, the Logos, and the disciple which was the theme of the preceding chapter. St. Paul's symbolism of the body and the head is replaced by a typology which has more support in the O.T. as it also had in contemporary Judaism of the non-rabbinical type:[1] in rabbinical literature it is comparatively rare, possibly because it was felt that the vine was not entirely free from heathen associations.[2]

The thought of the disciples as the friends of Jesus in 15. 15 and so in 16. 27 as friends of God represents a genuine adaptation of the Jewish theme that Abraham was the friend of God. But it is adapted to the Stoic theme that the wise man is not the suppliant but the friend of God in 16. 23,[3] where the disciples are told that when the Spirit has been sent they will not need to ask for anything; it is possible that the hatred of the world in 15. 18, which appears to replace the synoptic warning of coming persecution, is drawn from the belief that the true philosopher will be rejected and persecuted which goes back to Plato

[1] The grotesque Vine and Fountain of 2 Bar. 36. 1 ff. shows the vine as a recognized conventional symbol for Israel or the Messianic kingdom of which Israel is the centre. Cf. Cook, *Rel. Anc. Pal.* 193 f. and 212 f. for the use of the vine as a symbol (a Dionysiac influence going back to the Hasmoneans is suggested). Cf. also the vine in the synagogue frescoes of Doura-Europos (*The Excavations at Doura, Prel. Report of Sixth Season,* 367 ff.); Schürer, *G.J.V.* 2. 524, notes a synagogue of the vine at Sepphoris; Herod's vine on the Temple at Jerusalem (Jos. Antt. 15. 395, B.J. 5. 210) may have had a symbolic meaning, but was perhaps more probably a mere conventional decoration; Didache 9. 1 may perhaps go back independently to the vine as the symbol of Israel and the Messianic kingdom rather than to the Fourth Gospel. Behm in *T.W.z.N.T.*, s.voc., gives copious Mandean and pagan parallels but ignores Philo; Hoskyns and Davey (2. 560) rightly reject a direct borrowing from oriental mysticism; but the symbolism, though taken from the O.T., has been adapted to hellenistic forms of thought.

[2] Cf. Str.-B. on this passage.

[3] Cf. Seneca, Ep. 4. 2 (31) 8 ff. where the wise man 'incipit deorum socius esse, non supplex', since he is now 'deum in corpore humano hospitantem' just as the disciples in 17. 24 ff. are raised to a status superior to the world, described in language normally reserved for 'deification'; cf. below, p. 85, n. 1. For the thought cf. Philo, Fr. Barb. 6. 8 f. 101 in Wendland, *Neuentdeckte Fragm. Philos,* 55; it is interesting that here κελεύουσι καὶ προστάττουσι δούλοις δεσπόται, ἐντέλλονται δὲ φίλοι.

In De Somn. 1. 232 Philo holds that God can only appear talking as a friend to friends in the case of disembodied souls; it need hardly be said that elsewhere he describes Abraham and Moses as friends of God, e.g. De Abr. 273 where Abraham is the Stoic wise man, De Ebr. 94, Q.O.P.L. 43 where Moses as the wise man can actually be called a god (Exod. 7. 1, cf. p. 73, n. 3, and Lect. II, p. 36, n. 6), because he has God for his friend.

M

himself.¹ These are comparatively minor points; but the thought
of the Spirit as the ἔλεγχος in 16. 8 ff. is drawn from a range of ideas
well represented in Philo, for whom the conviction of sin arising
in the soul is 'no mean paraclete'.² He gives a long midrashic
exegesis on the law of leprosy in Lev. 13,³ where the living flesh
arising in the leprosy is a mark of uncleanness. This means that
the conviction of sin arising in the conscience proves that it is
alive and not dead. So in Lev. 14. 36 nothing is unclean in a
leper's house till the priest enters. This, says Philo, seems strange
to those who prefer the letter to the allegory; it ought to be
obvious that the soul is ignorant of sin and therefore innocent
until the divine Logos enters; it is when the true High Priest
ἔλεγχος enters the soul that it becomes guilty. The theme is
reinforced by 1 Kings 17. 10 ff., where the prophet who reminds
the widow of her sin is the word of God. Elsewhere ἔλεγχος can
be the Logos who meets Hagar, a friend and counsellor, the
High Priest of Num. 35. 25 on whose death the manslayer may
return to his sins;⁴ it can also be the true man who dwells in the
soul and guides it⁵ (we may compare the 'inner man' of 2 Cor.
4. 16); it can be the punisher set over the soul.⁶ Thus it has all
the functions of the paraclete as convincing the world of sin and
calling it to righteousness in the Fourth Gospel. Ἔλεγχος also
appears in Menander as the deified friend of truth,⁷ who must
be summoned as paraclete (παρακλητέος) to reinforce conscience;
he must be feared, for he will reveal all he knows of man. It
is also used of the Cynic philosopher⁸ who examines and convicts

¹ For the hellenistic view as coming from the Phaedrus (249 d) to the
Hermetica, cf. Kroll, op. cit. 383 f., and Corp. Herm. 9. 4 b.

² De Spec. Leg. 1. 237.

³ Q.D.S.I. 122 ff. The passage is notable for the very cavalier allusion to
literal exegetes in 133 and the non-pentateuchal references in 136 ff. which
suggest a Palestinian origin (cf. Note to Lect. II, p. 51 ff.); if this is so, it
would seem that a fairly advanced use of allegory was by no means confined to Alexandria.

⁴ De Fug. et Inv. 5 f. and 118.

⁵ Ib. 131, De Decal. 87, Q.D.P.I.S. 22 ff., and similar passages; cf. Bréhier,
Id. Phil. et. Rel. de Ph. 300, who points out their close resemblance to Polyb.
18. 43. 13, where σύνεσις replaces ἔλεγχος.

⁶ De Somn. 1. 91.

⁷ Ap. Lucian, Pseudol. 4 (3. 165), where he is the friend of truth and
παρρησία.

⁸ Cf. Epict. Diss. 1. 26. 17, and for other references cf. Büchsel, T.W.z.
N.T., s.voc. ἐλέγχω and Dio Chrys. Or. 8. 10, where men avoid Diogenes
for fear of ἔλεγχος. In Corp. Herm. 12 (1) 4 law appears as the punisher
and ἔλεγχος of evil-doers while in Exc. 27 (Scott, 1. 530) it brings man to the

the soul of man; thus it is easy for Philo to equate it with the prophets of the O.T. But it can also be a role of the Logos, and it was easy for the evangelist to transfer the term to the Holy Spirit.

This brings us to the culminating revelation; Jesus is about to depart from the disciples, but He will return to them with the coming of the paraclete and bring them the joy of free approach to the Father,[1] so that they will no longer need to ask questions of Jesus: they will only need ask the Father in His name and all will be revealed to them, for the Father loves them because they have believed that He came from God. And as He came from the Father into the world, so now He returns from the world to the Father. All this of course is specifically Christian, and expresses the normal theology of post-Pauline Christianity. But the passage (16. 25–8) as it stands is extremely obscure until we realize that it is the double function of the hellenistic prophet to reveal God to man and to forward man's prayers to God.[2] Since Jesus is more than a prophet, the dis-

desire of things which he did not know before. (Scott obelizes ἐπιθυμία and suggests ἐπιστήμη quite unnecessarily; it is quite reasonable that ἔλεγχος should bring man new desires; for ἐπιθυμία in a neutral sense cf. *T.W.z.N.T.*, s.voc.)

Büchsel, loc. cit., holds that the sense of 'reproving' or 'convicting' in the N.T. is drawn from the LXX and points out the similar development of the meaning of the word in Epictetus, ascribing the parallel development of the word to the predominantly ethical interest of Judaism on the one hand and Cynic philosophy on the other. But the sense goes back to Menander, and identification of ἔλεγχος as conscience with the Holy Spirit in this passage is entirely hellenistic.

[1] 16. 22 appears to conflate the two thoughts of the appearance of the risen Christ as bringing joy to the disciples and of the coming of the Spirit as bringing joy to the whole Church.

[2] Cf. Lucian, Alexander, 22 (2. 231), and for the language of Lucian here in relation to Christianity cf. p. 70, n. 1, and Fascher, Προφήτης, 203 ff. For the prophet as also a revealer cf. the scholiast on Aesch. Ag. 1099 quoted by Fascher, op. cit. 14, who explains προφήτας ᾿ οὕτινας ματεύομεν to mean τοὺς λέξοντας ἡμῖν περί σου· αὐτοὶ γὰρ αὐτόπται γινόμεθα. Here Jesus tells the disciples that He will no longer act as a hellenistic prophet explaining the truth to them ἐν παροιμίαις and forwarding their prayers to the Father; the Spirit which is to take His place will both reveal to the disciples the full truth and also enable them to ask the Father freely for all they need. This will be accomplished when Jesus returns to the Father, from whom He came; it is only then that He will be able to send down the Spirit, cf. above, p. 62, n. 2. For the whole passage cf. Corp. Herm. 13. 1 and 15.

(It should be noted that Fascher, op. cit. 203, makes the very unsafe assumption that Celsus' 'prophets' from Palestine can be quoted as parallels; the language of these prophets is merely Celsus' parody of perfectly good ante-Nicene Christian preaching of a rather enthusiastic type.)

ciples' recognition of His true nature carries with it the recognition that He knows all things and can reveal them without being questioned;[1] the evangelist seems to be following the tradition which is mentioned by Philo that the highest revelations are those which are given by God direct, as against those given in reply to the prophet's question; the same conception may be implied in the hermetic practice of substituting pure homiletic for the dialogue form as the revelation progresses.

The final interjection[2] paves the way for the High-priestly prayer. Here again the evangelist follows tradition, for a hellenistic revelation should conclude with a prayer which summarizes the content of the revelation and asks for grace to walk worthily of it. In this case the tradition determined that the prayer must be offered by Jesus, not by His disciples. Such revelations normally concern the relation of man to God as mediated by some more or less divine being, and the relation

---

[1] Verse 30 is taken by Holtzmann (*Joh.-Ev.* 283) to mean that Jesus knows the disciples' wishes before they are uttered; but ἐρωτᾶν here should mean to ask questions as in v. 23 (cf. Bauer, ad loc.). Bauer and Hoskyns and Davey leave this verse unexplained; Loisy regards it as marking the disciples' recognition of Jesus' omniscience, but does not explain why it should do so. The explanation in the text is based on Philo, De Vit. Moys. 2 (3), 189 ff.; he distinguishes between those parts of the Pentateuch which are the direct utterance of God and those which are mixed, since the prophet asks and God answers, the former being the higher. There seems no reason for this distinction, unless Philo is trying to drag in a bit of hellenistic erudition in his usual manner. The hermetic writings in their present form advance from the dialogue form to the homiletic or apocalyptic (1. 24 ff., 2. 13 ff., 4. 6 b ff., 10. 17 ff., where, however, Tat is allowed a final stupid question at 23; cf. also the concluding hymns of 13 and Ascl. 3). Whether the tendency is due to a desire to imitate the concluding myths of the Platonic dialogue or to the incapacity of the writers to keep up a dialogue form is another question; it seems at least possible that the evangelist was aware of a view that revelation in a set speech was higher than that in the form of dialogue, and so introduces it in a sentence which seems otherwise meaningless.

[2] It is generally held that Jesus' prophecy of the desertion of the disciples in 16. 32 ff. is intended to mark that their faith is still imperfect, cf. Hoskyns and Davey, ad loc. But this seems quite incompatible with the whole style of c. 17, especially of vv. 20 ff. It must be remembered that the prayer refers to the whole Church, not merely to the disciples at the particular moment, and the writer certainly does not regard the faith of the Church as a whole as imperfect. The prophecy of the failure of the disciples is simply due to the historical tradition, to which the author must do justice. Cf. 17. 8, where it is implied that the faith of the disciples is entirely adequate. Bauer notes that the prophecy is consistent with the synoptic story (Mk. 14. 50), but hardly with the implications of Jno. 18. 8 f.

of man both to God and to the cosmos which the revelation brings, as well as a prayer to persevere in the life and knowledge implied in the truths so revealed.[1] At one point indeed the language shows a parallel to Greek magical language which can hardly be accidental; in a papyrus the adept prays to Isis 'Glorify me, as I have glorified the name of thy son, (Horus)'.[2] The word Δόξα in the sense of glory appears to be purely Jewish in origin; in view of the rarity of

[1] Cf. Norden, *Agnostos Theos*, 111 ff., for speeches of this type; for specimens cf. Wisd. 9. 1 ff. (here the 'revelation' of c. 8 leads to a prayer; for the thought of 8. 20 cf. Corp. Herm. 10. 22 a, where the soul must pray that the 'mind' allotted to it may be a good one), Jos. Antt. 4, 315 ff., where Deut. 32 is transformed into a typical specimen (the prayer being for Israel, not for Moses himself, as it is for the disciples here), Corp. Herm. 1. 31 f., 5. 10 b, 13. 17, where the hymns are definitely associated with the unity of man with God and the cosmos in virtue of his possession of 'mind'; cf. further Ascl. 3. 41 b. Note especially ἅγιος ὁ θεός, ὃς γνωσθῆναι βούλεται καὶ γινώσκεται τοῖς ἰδίοις (1. 31), πιστεύω καὶ μαρτυρῶ ὅτι εἰς ζωὴν καὶ φῶς χωρῶ (ib. 32, cf. 13. 18), θέλησον ἡμᾶς Διατηρηθῆναι ἐν τῇ σῇ γνώσει καὶ φιλότητι (Ascl. 3. 41). In Exc. 23. 61 ff. Osiris and Isis cannot return from earth to heaven until they have called on the supreme God with a hymn which has not been preserved; here the parallel is very close, since the hymn is uttered not by man but by 'holy emanations' from God.

[2] P.M.G. 7. 503 ff. The words of the formula addressed to Isis Δόξασόν με ὡς ἐλόξασα τὸ ὄνομα τοῦ υἱοῦ σου Ὥρου are presumably a prayer for magical power, cf. 1. 209 ff., κατ' οὐρανὸν ἀνυψώθης καὶ κύριος ἐπεμαρτύρησεν τῇ σοφίᾳ σου καὶ κατευλόγησέν σου τὴν Δύναμιν καὶ εἶπέν σε σθένειν καθ' ὁμοιότητα αὐτοῦ ὅσον καὶ αὐτὸς σθένει. The latter passage reappears at 4. 1166 ff., conflated with a prayer to Helios-Aion (cf. Nock in *H.T.R.* 27. 1. 78 ff.). Here it is combined with Jewish elements which are easily separable. The first passage appears in a purely Graeco-Egyptian setting; 'Iao' does not appear between 495 and 595; the language of the second, where we have the same ideas but without Δόξα is distinctly Jewish, since all the words are common in LXX, except for σθένειν (5 times in LXX; 1 Pet. 5. 10; 7 times in Philo according to Leisegang's index). This might appear to tell against the view that Δόξα in the sense of 'glory' is of Jewish origin (cf. Kittel in *T.W.z.N.T.*, s.voc.). But as a rule the word in the papyri is used either of angels in a Jewish setting, or of the glory of God in the O.T. sense with a suggestion of personification, as in 4. 1201 ἐφώνησά σου τὴν ἀνυπέρβλητον Δόξαν (? Δόξαν) ὁ κτίσας Θεοὺς καὶ ἀγγέλους καὶ Δεκάνους· αἱ μυριάδες τῶν ἀγγέλων παρειστήκασί σοι; it is frequent in the 'Eighth Book of Moses' (Pap. 13. 78, 143, 189, 512, 591). [For the Jewish character of the Gnostic cosmogony underlying this papyrus cf. Dieterich, *Abraxas*, 70, 132 ff., and note the demand for 41 days' continence, i.e. Moses' forty days in Exod. 34. 28 with one added to avoid the risk of error, the opposite process to that of 'forty stripes save one' (cf. Str.-B. on 2 Cor. 11. 24).] Thus it would seem that the word passed from Jewish biblical and liturgical sources into magic and that in 7. 503 it has become sufficiently detached from its Jewish origins to figure in a purely heathen setting.

borrowings from Christianity in the magical papyri,[1] it is perhaps probable that both the magical prayer and the Johannine go back to Jewish prayers that God will glorify Israel as they have glorified Him, or His Wisdom, i.e. the Torah. The thought of the prayer itself is again purely Christian; it deals with love as the essential nature of the Father, uniting Him to the Son and both to the disciples, and the Cross as the revelation of the glory of God in Jesus. But the language again is hellenistic in its prayer that the disciples may have true gnosis and so possess eternal life, though gnosis is the Christian blend of faith and love, not mystical contemplation based on the literal observance and the allegorical interpretation of the Torah, as in Philo,[2] or with the knowledge of what passed for a system of philosophy, as in the Greek world.[3] Such gnosis involved detachment from the world, or at least from the material; the disciples here are already detached in virtue of their election,[4] (17. 14 ff.) yet Jesus prays that they may be preserved from the danger of falling away.[5] Gentiles, no less than Jews and Christians, were aware

[1] Apart from the well-known case in 4. 3019 'Jesus' appears as a magic word in 12. 192: cf. 12. 174, where the language of εὐχαριστῶ σοί, κύριε, ὅτι με ἔλυσεν τὸ πνεῦμα τὸ μονογενὲς τὸ ʒῶν looks Christian, cf. Jacoby, ad loc. For Jewish-hellenistic expositions of the theme suggested in the text cf. Ecclus. 36. 4 ff. (where v. 17 can mean 'Israel, whom thou hast made equal to thy first-born', i.e. to Wisdom = the Torah). Cf. also Ecclus. 1. 19, 4. 13, 42. 16, Wisd. 9. 10, 11. See also Reitzenstein, *Poimandres*, p. 22, n. 5.

[2] Philo does not seem to equate 'knowledge' and 'life' in so many words, but it is implied that they can be so identified in his favourite allegory of Nadab and Abihu, who attain to true life in God by fleeing from the material world and empty 'opinion' (Leg. Alleg. 2. 57; elsewhere they symbolize the flight from the material in the desire to attain to virtue). Cf. also De Post. Cain. 68, De Spec. Leg. 1. 31, De Gigant. 14. Naturally Philo holds that this 'life' cannot be attained without virtue. For the position of the Torah in the cosmos cf. De Mund. Op. 3, De Somn. 1. 36, where by implication it is identified with the music of the spheres.

[3] Corp. Herm. Ascl. 3. 41 b, 10. 15 a, Exc. 2 b 2. The nearest parallel would be 13. 8 b and 9 with Scott's excision of 8 c and the beginning of 9; but, apart from the question of the legitimacy of Scott's treatment of the text, here as elsewhere this tract has a suspiciously large number of resemblances to the N.T. which look like borrowings. Cf. Clem. Alex. Strom. 7. 3. 16 (837 P.), where the stamping of the image of the Logos on the soul of the Gnostic produces true life.

[4] For the world here cf. above, p. 57, n. 4. For the necessity for detachment from the material cf. Philo, Leg. Alleg. 3. 47; Q.D.P.I.S. 159; De Fug. et Inv. 59; De Somn. 2. 67 and *passim*.

[5] Cf. above, p. 79, n. 1. In Philo, De Virt. 182, the apostate immediately falls into every kind of vice. For a pagan view that relapse is impossible cf. Corp. Herm. 12 (1). 3; the view is clearly inconsistent with the prayers of 1.

of the danger that the convert (in the case of the Gentiles the convert to philosophy) might fall away, even though, like the Christians, they might seek to forestall the danger by roundly asserting that such a thing was impossible.[1]

(9) In the Passion narrative we are following an established tradition; the evangelist has some remarkable variations, due in part to his theology and in part perhaps to sources now lost; those which show hellenistic influence are not numerous. The most noticeable is the 'I am' of Jesus in Gethsemane, which makes His adversaries go back and fall to the ground. We have already noticed the importance of the formula; here it has a magical potency, which is somewhat startling.[2]

32 and Ascl. 3. 41 b. But St. Paul is equally inconsistent. Ro. 8. 5 implies that relapse is impossible for those who have the φρόνημα of the Spirit, but the purpose of the whole chapter is to encourage the reader to resist a real temptation. Heb. 6. 6 meets the difficulty by allowing that one relapse is possible; but such a relapse makes repentance impossible.

[1] For conversion to philosophy cf. Nock, Conversion, 164 ff. Naturally those trained in ethics by a life devoted to the study of philosophy would be less exposed to the danger of relapse than converts to the Church who had no Jewish or philosophical background. But Corp. Herm. 1. 26 b, 7. 1 a, and 13. 13 b show attempts at 'missionary' propaganda which if successful might well produce converts who were only half 'converted'. If such converts joined any kind of organized cult-society or sect of philosophy they would cause scandal if they fell away. Cf. Exc. 11. 4, where Tat is warned against the danger of talking with the ignorant for fear of ridicule, i.e. against indiscreet missionary zeal. In 10. 23 f. there is a warning that 'mind' is a gift of God, which may be withdrawn; in this case the soul sinks to the subhuman level. But the whole object of such tracts as the Poimandres is to rouse men to the knowledge that they are at least potential possessors of mind, and so to produce a conversion by 'mind'. The relapse of such a convert implies the withdrawal of the gift. Cf. Epict. Diss. 3. 15. 1 ff.

[2] Str.-B. on 18. 6 quote from Tanhuma a story of the officers sent by Joseph to arrest Symeon (Gen. 42. 24) falling down before him; the parallel would be interesting if it did not look suspiciously like a Jewish borrowing from the Fourth Gospel.

For the 'I am' formula cf. above p. 70, n. 1, p. 73, n. 3, and p. 78, n. 3. For the formula in pure magic cf. P.M.G. 12. 228 ff., where the magician identifies himself with a whole number of deities including Isis and Osiris and also 'Faith'; it is surprising not to find Iao. In 5. 110 he proclaims his identity with Moses; in 147 he proclaims ἐγώ εἰμι ἡ ἀλήθεια an apparently startling resemblance to Jno. 14. 6, which is purely accidental, since the papyrus refers to Maāt, the Egyptian goddess of truth (Preisendanz, Akephalos, 43). Cf. also 5. 248 ff., 7. 325 ff., and see Dieterich, Abraxas, 25, n. 2. The most interesting parallel is in P.M.G. 13. 254 ff., ἐγώ εἰμι ὁ ἐπὶ τῶν Δύο χερυβεὶν ἀνὰ μέσον τῶν Δύο φύσεων οὐρανοῦ καὶ γῆς, ἡλίου τε καὶ σελήνης, φωτὸς καὶ σκότους· φάνηθί μοι ὁ ἀρχάγγελος τῶν ὑπὸ τὸν κόσμον, αὐθέντα Ἥλιε ὁ ὑπὸ αὐτὸν τὸν ἕνα καὶ μόνον

The dialogue with Pilate abandons the synoptic tradition in order to introduce Jesus as the king who has come into the world from a higher sphere; since God Himself can be a king, it follows that His Logos can also be so described.[1] But Pilate ignores the proclamation of the divine origin of Jesus with a piece of empty cynicism, which identifies him with the conventional persecutor of the Church;[2] it is only when he is told

τεταγμένος· προστάσσει σοὶ ὁ ἀεὶ καὶ μόνος. Here the magician has the precise character of the Logos in such passages as Philo, De Fug. et Inv. 101 ff. (contrast De Cher. 24, where the function is reserved for God Himself, i. e. Iao; for this passage cf. Gentiles, 46, n. 5). Similarly in P.M.G. 4. 1117 ff. we find a spirit which penetrates from earth to heaven and might come either from Wisd. 8. 1 or from the Stoic models of that passage. In the former passage we have a genuine religion of a mixed Jewish and Gentile character centred on the sun; for more or less monotheistic solar cults cf. Cumont, Rel. Or. 66, 106, and 123, and Nock, Conversion, 118 and 134 f. Cf. also Pausanias, 7. 23. 7, where a priest of Sidon describes Apollo as the sun and Asclepius as the air, as being the source of health; here Asclepius (=Baal-Eshmun) is a Logos in the sphere of health subject to Apollo as the sun (whether Zeus was above Apollo as the aether does not appear). See also Corp. Herm. 16. 5 for the sun as a demiurge-Logos and Macr. Sat. 1. 23. 21. In P.M.G. 13. 254 genuine religion has degenerated into magic, but its original character remains clear.

Norden, Agnostos Theos, 194 ff. treats the 'I am' of Mk. 14. 62 as a proclamation of this type, which if genuine would imply that Jesus was a 'prophet' of the type described by Celsus; for these cf. p. 83, n. 2 above. But the logion if genuine need be no more than an affirmative reply to the High Priest's question. On the other hand, it is highly probable that both Mt. and Lk. felt that the phrase was open to objection on the ground of its magical associations and changed it for that reason.

[1] In Philo, De Agric. 50, the title of shepherd is so noble that it can be applied nor merely to kings and wise men and souls that are perfectly cleansed but even to God Himself (cf. above, p. 83, n. 2). In De Mut. Nom. 116 mind treats the divine Logos as its shepherd and king. Thus Jesus as the Logos is a king; but the language may be partly inspired by the belief that kings were drawn from the highest strata of the cosmos, reserved for the highest class of souls, so that a king could be said to 'come into' the world in a special sense. (Cf. Corp. Herm. Exc. 23. 42, 26. 1 and 8 ff., where particular deities are 'kings' of particular departments of existence, Osiris of the dead, Hermes of teaching, &c., which appears to be a combination of the belief that most of the gods were kings who had attained to immortality (Diod. Sic. 1. 13. 1), with the belief that the gods are logoi of particular aspects of life and the cosmos.) The same belief could be applied to the soul of the wise man, cf. Philo, Q. in Gen. 3. 10, De Gig. 12 ff. and passim, Dio Chrys. Or. 30. 27 of the heroes of antiquity.

[2] The average Roman magistrate regarded the refusal of the Christian to acknowledge the divinity of the Emperor as a futile piece of perverse obstinacy (Pliny, Ad Tra. 96. 3; Mart. Polyc. 8. 2, 9. 2; Tert. ad Nat. 1. 17; Minucius, Oct. 8. 5), while to the Christian the refusal of the magistrate

that Jesus claims to be the Son of God that we hear that he was 'more afraid'. There is of course no reason to suppose that the historical Pilate would either have understood the meaning of Jesus' claim to a supernatural kingship or been impressed by hearing that He claimed to be a θεοῦ παῖς; there is no reason to suppose that he was in any way interested in religion. The evangelist, however, has both to represent Pilate as the cynical disbeliever, who is none the less overawed by the divine epiphany, and yet to leave to the Jews the greater share of guilt for the crucifixion, and to do it within the very narrow limits of the historical tradition; it must be recognized that he has done it with remarkable success. The Resurrection narrative again shows no trace of hellenistic influence apart from its allusion to the Gentile Churches as those who have not seen and yet have believed.

I have endeavoured to suggest one, but only one, of the main elements out of which the Fourth Gospel is made up. There are at least two others, the older Christian tradition and Jewish rabbinical theology. The greatness of the Gospel lies in the fact that while it interprets the life of Jesus in terms of the theology of the age, it never loses sight of the concrete historical figure of the synoptic tradition or of love as the distinctive quality of Christianity.[1] There are moments when it comes dangerously

to be drawn into a debate on Christian apologetics seemed to be a cynical disregard of the truth. Cf. Tert. Apol. 1; and the attempts of the martyrs to draw the magistrates into discussion in the Acts of Carpus and Papylus (Owen, *Acts of the Early Martyrs*, 42 ff.), the Scillitan Martyrs (ib. 71 f.), and Procopius (ib. 128). Geffcken (*Zwei griechische Apologeten*, 246 ff.) appears to regard all such attempts of the martyrs to enter into a discussion of apologetics as unhistorical on the ground that they deal mainly in the commonplaces of literary apologetics. But it seems not unlikely that the ordinary Christian heard enough of the popular arguments which form the stock-in-trade of the apologists to be able to use them on the most inappropriate occasions; after all, such arguments may well have played a considerable part in the homiletics of the primitive Church. It may be doubted whether the theme would have been so popular in the literary Acts, if it had not a considerable basis in fact, though it is naturally probable that the present form of such arguments is derived largely from the conventional apologetic literature.

[1] For ἀγάπη as a distinctively Christian development of the O.T. conception cf. Stauffer in *T.W.z.N.T.*, s.voc. It may be noted that it does not figure very prominently in Philo, and that when it appears it is always drawn from his O.T. sources. Thus De Post. Cain. 69 = Deut. 30. 19: De Spec. Leg. 1. 300 = Deut. 10. 12, De Migr. Abr. 21 alludes to the same passage, as does Q.D.S.I. 69 (note the association of love and fear); De Cher. 73 is drawn from Exod. 21. 5. In De Migr. Abr. 169 the command to the soul to ascend to God ἀγαπητικῶς is drawn from the fact that Abihu means 'my

near to presenting Jesus as a purely docetic epiphany on the stage of history, but these are always corrected by the evangelist's fidelity to the main Christian tradition. A comparison with the apocryphal Gospels of the second Christian century reveals the dangers that beset him and the masterly skill with which he avoided them.[1]

NOTE I

Regeneration

It was a matter of common form in primitive initiation rites that the initiate underwent a new birth (cf. Frazer, *The Golden Bough, The Magic*

father'; the relative correctness of the translation of Nadab ($=$ ἑκούσιος) and Abihu here shows that Philo is drawing on a source which is more in contact with Jewish than with Greek thought. De Abr. 50 draws its use of love from the fact that Abraham is the friend of God, while De Fug. et Inv. 114 is inspired by the use of the High Priest's marriage as a symbol for the relation of the soul to God. Josephus' use in such passages as Antt. 7. 269 betrays his inability to dissociate himself from his Jewish upbringing even when he is trying to write in a Greek convention. Διάνοια τὸ θεῖον ἀγαπῶσα is a shocking hybrid.

[1] If the views put forward above are accepted, it would seem to follow that the date of the Fourth Gospel can hardly be earlier than about A.D. 90. But it is possible that the resemblances between this Gospel and the Pauline Epistles including the post-Pauline Ephesians are due not to borrowing but to a common use of the accepted language and outlook of first-century Christianity, in which case the Gospel might be dated some twenty or thirty years earlier. Similarly while I have assumed that the arguments between the Church and the synagogue reflect the situation at Ephesus, in view of the strong traditional association of the Gospel with that city, it is perfectly possible that such arguments should have begun at Antioch.

The *terminus ante quem* for the composition of the Gospel is provided (*a*) by the Rylands Library fragment published by C. H. Roberts (*An Unpublished Fragment of the Fourth Gospel in the Rylands Library*), dated on palaeographic grounds to the first half of the second century. The editor allows a probable time-lag of thirty years between the writing of the Gospel and its copying in Egypt. (*b*) By P. Egerton 2 (*Fragments of an Unknown Gospel*, ed. Bell and Skeat). In spite of the objections of the editors (pp. 35 ff.) I find it quite impossible to suppose that the compiler of this document is not compiling a midrash on at least one of the Synoptic Gospels and the Fourth Gospel; the differences between him and the Fourth Gospel seem to be due to the fact that he knows it by heart, though somewhat inaccurately, and has inserted fragments of it to suit his purpose. If this view is correct, we have evidence of the wide diffusion of the Gospel and its acceptance as more or less 'canonical scripture' by A.D. 150. This certainly demands a time-lag of thirty years, and even this is very short.

On the whole it seems difficult, though not impossible, to date the Gospel before A.D. 90. Any date after A.D. 100 involves great difficulty, rising to impossibility by A.D. 120.

Art, 1. 74 ff., James: *Origins of Sacrifice,* c. v., and see the biblio-graphy to that chapter). On the other hand, the conception was alien to Judaism. Köhler attempts to read it into such sayings as that a proselyte is like a new-born babe (*Jewish Encyclopedia,* art. 'Birth, The New'), but the emphasis in such passages is not on the fact that he has become a new kind of person, but that he has been freed from his previous obligations (cf. *Judaism,* 1. 334). Köhler, loc. cit., holds that the dialogue of Jno. 3. 3 ff. misrepresents Judaism, since Nicode-mus would have understood the allusion quite easily. This is probable enough; but the importance of the passage lies in the light which it throws on the controversy between the Church and the synagogue towards the end of the first century A.D. Christianity maintains the need of a 'new birth' through baptism; Judaism rejects the idea as ridiculous. (Odeberg's suggestion that the allusion here is not to baptism but to the procreative power of the Spirit (*The Fourth Gospel,* 48) is quite untenable; if the words ἐξ ὕδατος are part of the original text (there is no MS. evidence for their excision, cf. Hoskyns and Davey, ad loc.), no Christian reader could have understood them except as an allusion to baptism; if they are a later insertion, we still have to explain the interpretation of conversion as a 'new birth' instead of a death and resurrection, as they are to St. Paul; and the separation of conversion and baptism would have been meaningless to a Christian of the first century.)

It is natural to suppose that we have here the influence of 'mystery-cults'; but it is very hard to find any very clear evidence that the idea of regeneration figured prominently in them. The most often quoted parallel is Apuleius, Metam. 11. 16 (785) and 24 (806). But the first passage refers not to Lucius' regeneration by initiation but to his 'new birth' by his miraculous restoration to human form; here Apuleius appears to apologize for the word by adding 'quodam modo'. After initiation he celebrates 'festissimum natalem sacrorum', but it is diffi-cult to see that the description of his initiation as a 'birthday' implies that the rite was habitually interpreted as a 'new birth'; the account of it implies that it was rather an approach to death in the form of a visit to the lower world and a more or less miraculous return (ib. 23. 804). Nor is it clear that the *Taurobolium* was regarded as conveying a 'new birth' until a considerably later period. It was in any case a public act, not an initiation (Nock, *Conversion,* 69); and it appears to have been a rite performed on behalf of the State as well as on behalf of individuals, and the first description of its recipient as 'renatus in aeter-num' dates from the Julianic revival (Nock in *C.A.H.* 12. 424).

Apart from these cases the allusions to 'regeneration' in pre-Christian literature are neither numerous nor striking. Professor A. D. Nock in Rawlinson, *Essays on the Trinity and the Incarnation,* 117, adds a few doubtful cases. Bauer on Jno. 3. 3 asserts that the conception of regeneration grew up on syncretistic soil, and quotes Ps.-Plat.

Axiochos 731 d for γεννητὸς τῶν θεῶν: apart from the stock instances already considered he adds a large number of parallels from post-Christian Gnostics and the equally post-Christian Hermetica. The former are not evidence in so far as they may be drawn from the ortho-dox Christian view; and the main hermetic evidence is the curious tract Corp. Herm. 13, where Tat undergoes 'a curious sacrament of auto-suggestion, in which the powers of evil are driven out of a man and the powers of good take their place' (Nock, *Conversion*, 12). In view of the extent to which this tract is used as an argument for the view that belief in regeneration by mysteries was widely spread in the hellenistic world, it must be noted that Scott, 2. 374, regards this tract as one of the latest; it must be added that it is unusually full of phrases which suggest Christian influence. (Cf. also Nock in *Journal of Egyptian Archaeology*, xv. 3 and 4 (1929), 232, for its similarity to certain aspects of the magical papyri.)

Thus the title alludes to a 'mountain' on which the discourse is delivered and in 1 the corrupt phrase ἐπὶ τῆς τοῦ ὄρους μεταβάσεως (? τῆς ἀπὸ τοῦ ὄρους καταβάσεως) implies that Hermes has delivered a previous discourse on a mountain somewhere. Scott, ad loc., supposes that he has 'taken Tat up to the desert plateau above the Nile valley'. But the proper place for an Egyptian revelation is not a mountain in the desert but a temple (cf. Corp. Herm. Ascl. 3. 1 b, the pagan Therapeutae and κάτοχοι (for these see Cumont, *L'Ég. d. Astr.* 147 and the literature quoted there); the Hostanes story in Ps.-Democritus, for which see Cumont and Bidez, *Les Mages Hellénisées*, 2. 317; the Mandulis vision discussed by Nock in *H.T.R.* 27. 1. 55 ff. ('A Vision of Mandulis-Aion'); and the revelation of Thessalus, Catal. Codd. Ast. 8. 4. 253 ff., where a temple is clearly implied). On the other hand, for Judaism or Christianity a mountain is obviously the correct scene for a revelation; the phrase here distinctly suggests 2 Pet. 1. 19. Apart from this there are a number of very suspicious points.

(*a*) ἀπηλλοτρίωσα τὸ ἐν ἐμοὶ φρόνημα ἀπὸ τῆς τοῦ κόσμου ἀπάτης. Here the language as to alienation may be common form, cf. the Mandulis inscription, Nock, loc. cit., ἀλλότριον ἐμαυτὸν ἐποιησάμην ἀπὸ πάσης κακίας καὶ πάσης ἀθεότητος, and Vettius Valens, 5. 9 (240. 27) πάσης ἡδονῆς καὶ κολακείας ἀλλοτριωθέντες as the benefit to be won by the study of astrology. But while it is natural to be alienated from sin or the material as a result of or a means of attaining to the new birth (cf. 1 Pet. 2. 1), it is very startling to find the cosmos identified with evil except in Christian writings, where it is common form. (Cf. esp. 1 Jno. 2. 15 ff.)

(*b*) In the same section τὰ ὑστερήματα ἀναπλήρωσον is very Pauline, cf. Col. 1. 24, 2 Cor. 9. 12, while ἐξ οἵας μήτρας, σπορᾶς δὲ ποίας might quite well be borrowed from Nicodemus in Jno. 3. 4.

(*c*) In 2 the θέλημα of God as the agent of regeneration is suspiciously reminiscent of the N.T. (Gal. 1. 4, Eph. 1. 5), the more so as the word

in this sense appears to be Jewish-Christian and to have reached the
hermetica via the LXX. (Cf. Schrenk in *T.W.z.N.T.* 3. 53 f. In *Voc.
Gr.N.T.* the word is regarded as 'practically unknown outside bibl. and
eccl. writings'; the only parallels quoted are from papyri under LXX
influence, but the word appears about three times in the sense of wish
or impulse, cf. Schrenk, loc. cit.) For the θέλημα of God cf. 1 Pet. 3.
17; the word might easily have been used in the place of the Logos or
God as the agent of regeneration in 1 Pet. 1. 23. That the person re-
born becomes the son of God may be common form, but cf. Jno. 1. 12;
'this kind is not taught' might well be a verbal echo of Mk. 9. 29.

(*d*) In 3 Scott alters ἀλλότριος υἱὸς πέφυκα τοῦ πατρικοῦ γένους by
insererting ἄρα and omitting υἱὸς to make an iambic line 'presumably
quoted from some play'; but the words might quite well be a reminiscence of Ps. 69. 9, a regular Psalm of the Passion in Christian apologetics (Lk. 23. 36; Jno. 2. 17 and 19. 29). That the regeneration should
take place ἐξ ἐλέου θεοῦ (cf. 7*b*) suggests the N.T. (1 Cor. 7. 25; 1 Tim.
1. 13 and 16; 1 Pet. 2. 10). The conception of the regenerate being
as different from the being seen with the natural eye has at least
a considerable affinity with the docetic belief of such passages as Acts
of John 89 ff., in which the conception is natural as an attempt to
explain the person of Jesus, whereas here it seems to have no real
point.

(*e*) In 4 the description of the author of regeneration as ὁ τοῦ θεοῦ
παῖς ἄνθρωπος εἷς θελήματι θεοῦ. Scott omits ὁ τοῦ transferring the whole
to 2. If Scott's emendation be accepted, the words mean that a man
who is 'a son of God' is needed to effect regeneration, which might
have been altered into ὁ τοῦ by a Christian. Even so, the words have
a suspiciously Christian ring, which might be due to a deliberate imitation of Christianity.

(*f*) In 5 the 'mortal form' which 'changes from day to day' may
be a mere commonplace (cf. Exc. 2*a* 10), but is very like 2 Cor. 4. 16.

(*g*) In 6 δοκοῦντός μου ὑπὸ σοῦ σοφοῦ γεγονέναι suggests Ro. 1. 22 and
1 Cor. 3. 18.

(*h*) In 7*b* and 8*a* we find ἔλεος again with a very Jewish Christian
colouring, cf. (*d*) above and also Justin Martyr, Dial. c. Tryph. 8 (226*b*),
where we have a formal summary of the requirements of Judaism ending καὶ τότε σοι ἴσως ἔλεος ἔσται παρὰ θεοῦ. It is at least possible that
the hermetic phrase is taken from a Jewish or Christian formula summarizing the demands imposed on the prospective convert and the
benefits he may hope for.

(*i*) In 9 Scott recognizes that Δικαιοσύνη and ἐΔικαιώθημεν are probably due to Pauline influence at second-hand. The words βαθμός and
ἕΔρασμα may be an echo of the language though not the thought of
1 Tim. 3. 13 ff., with ἕΔρασμα substituted for the rare ἑΔραίωμα. Naturally
no argument can be based on 'truth', 'light', and 'life' at the end of
this section.

(*k*) The same applies to such terms as γνῶσις and φωτισθείς in 18; but cf. Scott for the Jewish affinities of the hymn.

(1) In 22 *a* καρποφορήσοντος has Christian associations (Col. 1. 6 and 10). The 'immortal γενήματα of truth' (for the spelling cf. *Voc. Gr. N.T.* s.voc.; the form γένημα is required by the metaphor of fruit-bearings) might come from 2 Cor. 9. 10 = Hos. 10. 12.

In view of the similarities noted, it seems perilous to use this tract as evidence of Christian borrowing from 'syncretistic' surroundings; it looks as though the borrowing were on the hermetic side. The 'Mithras-Liturgy' (P.M.G. 4. 646) contains the phrase σήμερον τούτου ὑπὸ σοῦ μεταγεννηθέντος, but again the date of this is quite uncertain.

It is also quite impossible to trace any real connexion between the Christian conception of regeneration and Philo, De Cher. 40 ff. and similar passages (cf. above, Lect. I, note I, for this passage, which seems entirely dictated by the need of finding an allegorical meaning for the curious fact that the O.T. does not state that Abraham, Isaac, Jacob, and Moses 'knew' their wives, as it does in the case of Adam). On the other hand, in Q. in Exod. 2. 46 (A. 502) we are told that 'Sursum vocatio prophetae secunda est nativitas (sive regeneratio) priore melior; illa enim commixta per carnem etiam corruptibiles habebat parentes; ista vero incommixta simplexque anima principalis, mutata ad ingenitam cuius non est mater; sed pater solus, qui etiam universorum.' This explains why in Exod. 24. 16 the mountain is covered with cloud for six days, the number of creation, but Moses goes up on the seventh day.

Philo's thought would exactly fit the situation in Jno. 3, since every Christian, certainly any 'master in Israel', ought to be 'sursum vocatus'. It is possible that Philo's conception was derived from the general outlook of the hellenistic world as conditioned by the growth of mystery-cults. But the evidence for the prevalence of such views in the sophisticated cults of the hellenistic age is almost entirely post-Christian, and the connexion between such later conceptions and the primitive beliefs of savage initiation-cults as to the 'rebirth' of the initiate on the occasion of his passage into manhood is by no means clear. It would rather seem that the growth of interest in such cults and their increased emphasis on personal religion as against the older cults of the city-states was leading at the beginning of the first century A.D. to the independent development in various cults and in the theology which explained them to such metaphors as that of 'regeneration', and that Philo, the Fourth Gospel, and 1 Peter are simply instances of that process in the hellenistic-Jewish and Christian world. It is of course possible that the rabbinical language noted above represents an earlier belief in the 'regeneration' of the proselyte watered down in view of the growth of Christianity. It is also possible that the fashion ultimately went back to the language of one or other of those cults which had preserved a formula of 'regeneration' from the days when it really was the initiation-rite of a primitive clan, tribe, or people.

LECTURE I: ADDITIONAL NOTE

For the stories of escape from prison in the Acts cf. Weinreich, *Gebet u. Wunder* in *Tüb. Beitr. z. Alt.-Wiss.* 5. 313 ff. He suggests that we have (*a*) a non-miraculous story of the deliverance of Peter and John (Acts 4. 21) and (*b*) three miraculous deliverances of 'the Apostles' (5. 19), Peter (12. 1 ff.) and Paul and Silas (16. 25 ff.); thus we get an instance of the 'Rule of three' common in popular literature. But it is very doubtful whether we can class four deliverances, of which only three are miracles, as an instance of this; there should be either three miracles or one natural and two miraculous deliverances. Further, there should be a steady enhancement of the miraculous element as the story grows, whereas Peter's deliverance is definitely more miraculous than that of Paul and Silas. His attempt to trace from the language of Acts a definite influencing of the story by the Bacchae of Euripides is interesting but scarcely convincing; it seems far more likely that stories of this very favourite type tended to be told in language which ultimately goes back to Euripides, rather than that the author of Acts was himself influenced by the Bacchae, although the possibility cannot be ruled out. In any case it seems more probable that Paul and Silas had a deliverance of a striking character, which acquired a miraculous colouring, than that we have simply a third miraculous version of the story of Acts 4. 21.

INDEXES

I. GREEK AND LATIN WRITERS

O

II. JEWISH WRITERS

III. OLD TESTAMENT

IV. NEW TESTAMENT

V. CHRISTIAN WRITERS

VI. MODERN WRITERS

VII. NAMES AND SUBJECTS

PRINTED IN GREAT BRITAIN AT THE UNIVERSITY PRESS, OXFORD
BY JOHN JOHNSON, PRINTER TO THE UNIVERSITY